UNDERGROUND, *MONROE*, AND *THE MAMALOGUES*

UNDERGROUND, MONROE, AND THE MAMALOGUES

THREE PLAYS

Lisa B. Thompson

Foreword by E. Patrick Johnson
Interview with Joan Morgan

Northwestern University Press
Evanston, Illinois

Northwestern University Press
www.nupress.northwestern.edu

Printed in the United States of America

10 9 8 7 6 5 4 3 2 1

Library of Congress Cataloging-in-Publication Data

Names: Thompson, Lisa B., 1965– author. | Morgan, Joan, 1965– interviewer. | Johnson, E. Patrick, 1967– writer of foreword. | Thompson, Lisa B., 1965–. Underground. | Thompson, Lisa B., 1965–. Monroe. | Thompson, Lisa B., 1965–. Mamalogues.
Title: Underground, Monroe, and The Mamalogues : three plays / Lisa B Thompson, with a foreword by E. Patrick Johnson.
Description: Evanston, Illinois : Northwestern University Press, 2020.
Identifiers: LCCN 2020009284 | ISBN 9780810142275 (paperback) | ISBN 9780810142282 (ebook)
Subjects: LCSH: African Americans—Drama. | LCGFT: Drama.
Classification: LCC PS3620.H68347 A6 2020 | DDC 812/.6—dc23
LC record available at https://lccn.loc.gov/2020009284

For my siblings, Debra, Guy, and Robert.
And for black girls everywhere with stories to tell.

CONTENTS

FOREWORD

E. Patrick Johnson

It is one thing to read a play on the page. It is quite another to embody one of the characters from a play onstage. In 2015, I had the pleasure of playing the role of Mason in Lisa B. Thompson's *Underground* in a staged reading at the American Studies Association conference in Toronto. Kyle was played by my colleague and fellow thespian Marlon M. Bailey. Bailey and I had longed to share the stage and this play had provided that occasion. While performing in a staged reading at an academic conference might sound like a torturous experience to some, for me it was thrilling to watch an audience—even an academic one—engage the three-dimensional characters that Thompson had created. What became evident over the course of the reading is that these two characters whose politics and motivations seem polar opposite are actually more alike than they care to admit. As the audience learns more about Kyle and Mason, therefore, their sympathies shift between the two, for each character's integrity is called into question at different moments over the course of the play as their secrets and lies are exposed.

As with the characters in *Underground*, the characters in the other plays collected in this volume are always more than they appear on the surface. Like a good tea, they become more complex the more they simmer and steep. And as these characters' stories emerge, so too, does the political commentary about the world in which they and we live. For Thompson that world is decidedly black and most often middle-class. The focus on the black middle class in these plays is less about black triumphalism than it is about the slippages and foibles of such a class position. Moreover, Thompson's characters are not deemed inherently politically compromised or deserving of their troubles because of their class status; rather, they are shown to grapple with the constants of racism, sexism, misogyny, and homophobia despite ascending to the middle class.

Writing in the tradition of a long line of black female playwrights from the early twentieth century, such as Angelina Weld Grimké and Georgia Douglas, to contemporary authors, such as Pearl Cleage, Lydia Diamond, Lynn Nottage, and Dael Orlandersmith, Thompson culls her talents as artist, scholar, and activist to engage the lives of black folk through a decidedly feminist lens. Even when all of the characters in her plays are male—as is the case with *Underground*—Thompson's critique of the trappings of patriarchy and masculinity shines through. In *Monroe*, a play that is sympathetic toward the plight of black men who are the victims of lynching, the story line is equally about the toll lynching takes on black women who are left in the wake of persistent black death. And through at times slapstick humor, *The Mamalogues* wages a deft critique of heteropatriarchy and the systemic effects it has on black middle-class women who are also single mothers.

As a "holy trinity" of indefatigable, insightful, and inspirational plays, this collection encourages us to check the assumptions we make based on superficial indicators. Indeed, these plays compel us to engage the whole person—as human—such that we ourselves can become more human in the other's eyes.

ACKNOWLEDGMENTS

The publication of *Underground*, *Monroe*, and *The Mamalogues* in one volume brings me great joy. When I moved to Austin in 2012, I found a vibrant theater community that embraced me and my work. I'm fortunate that these plays had world premieres at two of the most dynamic theater companies in Texas: the Austin Playhouse and The Vortex. I'm profoundly grateful to Lara Toner, artistic director of the Austin Playhouse, for directing a gorgeous production of *Monroe* in the South, where it belongs, which surely pleased my Louisiana ancestors. I remain in awe of Bonnie Cullum, artistic director and the force behind The Vortex. She believed in *Underground* and ensured that my vision was realized. As I write this, Bonnie and Christine Hoang, my sister playwright and enterprising Color of Arc Productions artistic director, are bringing *The Mamalogues* to The Vortex stage. I'm especially grateful to the brilliant and generous Rudy Ramirez for introducing me to The Vortex family and for his imaginative direction of both *Underground* and *The Mamalogues*.

New play development can be a daunting task, but it's easier when you work with amazing directors. Tim Bond, Marcus McQuirter, and Isaiah Wooden directed staged readings of the plays in this collection and I benefited greatly from their brilliance and generosity. Colman Domingo is my most frequent collaborator and one of my dearest friends. He has directed workshops and readings of all of my plays. Colman showed me how to walk into a rehearsal room with intention, openness, and care, and I'm eternally grateful for that lesson. I have also been fortunate to work with a host of exceptionally talented actors, each of whom left their imprint on these plays during workshops, readings, and productions. I'm grateful to them all.

While the theater community is essential, as a black feminist cultural producer and critic my intellectual community is equally important. The

University of Texas at Austin's African and African Diaspora Studies Department is a rich and supportive environment. I also benefit from my affiliations with the John L. Warfield Center for African and African American Studies, the Center of Women and Gender Studies, the English Department, and the Department of Theatre and Dance. I'm grateful to my friends and colleagues Bedour Alagraa, Abimbola Adelakun, Charles Anderson, Tony Araguz, Jossiana Arroyo-Martínez, Daina Ramey Berry, Jackson Brown, Keffrelyn Brown, Simone Browne, Nicole Burrowes, Charlotte Canning, Ashley Farmer, Kevin Foster, Shaleiah Fox, Lyndon Gill, Edmund T. Gordon, Kali Gross, Frank Guridy, Susan Heinzelman, Robert Jensen, Peniel Joseph, Stephanie Lang, Xavier Livermon, Kirk Lynn, Justice Madden, Minkah Makalani, Stephen Marshall, Gesel Mason, Elizabeth McCracken, Lisa Moore, Deborah Paredes, Samantha Pinto, Abena Dove Osseo-Assare, Robert Ramirez, Carlos Ramos, Richard Reddick, Roger Reeves, Judith Rhedin, Matt Richardson, Rebecca Rossen, Ann H. Stevens, Pauline Strong, Cherise Smith, Eric Tang, Shirley Thompson, Omiseke Tinsley, João Vargas, Jennifer Wilks, Helena Woodard, and Hershini Bhana Young for their support. I'm especially grateful to Omi Osun Joni L. Jones for welcoming me and for insisting on a place for black theater and performance at UT Austin. I will never forget how Randy Diehl, the former Dean of the College of Liberal Arts, championed my work as both an artist and a scholar.

I have been the receipeint of generous support from a variety of institutions. I developed these plays in residence at the W. E. B. Du Bois Research Institute at the Hutchins Center for African & African American Research, the Millay Colony for the Arts, Hedgebrook, and the Humanities Institute at the University of Texas at Austin. I have received funding from the John L. Warfield Center for African and African American Studies and ScriptWorks. I appreciate Marcyliena Morgan, executive director of the HipHop Archive and Research Institute at Harvard; Ralina Joseph, director of the Center for Communication, Difference, and Equity at the University of Washington, Seattle; Anthony Stewart of Bucknell University; Pauline Strong of UT Austin's Humanities Institute; and the National Women's Studies Association for inviting me to present readings of *The Mamalogues*. I'm grateful to Langdon Brown of the New York State Writers Institute, and to the American Studies Association for hosting staged readings of *Under-*

ground. As I developed these plays and assembled this collection, I relied on my diligent and knowledgeable student research assistants: Nyesha Brown, Deanna Howard, Christina Knight, Michael Love, Gabrielle Randall, and Phillip Townsend. This book would not be in print without the vision, dedication, and leadership of former and current Northwestern University Press staff: Olivia Aguilar, Jane Bunker, Anne Gendler, Parneshia Jones, Gianna Mosser, Jill Petty, Patrick Samuel, Courtney Smotherman, and Anne Tappan Strother.

My friends have showed up for me in so many important ways, including giving me notes on scenes, attending a staged reading, recommending my plays to artistic directors, or flying across the country to see a performance. I'm thankful to Angela Antonikowski, Angela Ards, Sandra Austin, Dean Bachus, Marlon Bailey, Stephanie Batiste, Herman Beavers, Lisa Coronado, Curtis Bonney, Daphne Brooks, Langdon Brown, Scott Paulson Bryant, Deidre Hill Butler, Faedra Carpenter, David Campt, Adrienne Childs, James Corbett, Valisa Dougherty, Augustus I. Durham, Harry J. Elam Jr., Michele Elam, Shirley Jo Finney, Nicole Fleetwood, Dan Floyd, Henry Louis Gates Jr., Vera Grant, Tera Hunter, David Ikard, Maricella Infante, Daniel Alexander Jones, Meta DuEwa Jones, Stephen Liacourus, Elizabeth Lauenstein, Treva Lindsey, Betelhem Makonnen, Tracy Manier, Dwight A. McBride, Scott Million, Mark Anthony Neal, Marisol Negron, Jeremy O'Brian, Sophie Oldfield, Diana Paulin, Kathy Perkins, Skip Quaities, Dion Raymond, Guthrie Ramsey, Sonnet Retman, Jennifer Richmond, Rita Rothman, Tammie Rubin, Tracy Scacutto, Ron Simons, Darieck Scott, Evie Shockley, Valerie Smith, Maury Sullivan, Fatima Washington, Omar Wasow, Marco Williams, and Lisa Woolfork. I'm grateful to my sister theater artists, playwrights, directors, and performance artists, who sustain and inspire me: Florinda Bryant, Sharon Bridgforth, Donnetta Lavinia Grays, Virginia Grise, Jeanette Hill, Chisa Hutchinson, Jacqueline Lawton, Christi Moore, Dominique Morisseau, Naomi Wallace, and Sharon Washington. I'm especially thankful to Cherríe Moraga, whose invitation to join a playwriting group in San Francisco when I was a graduate student changed the trajectory of my life.

Four angels blessed this play collection with their unique gifts. I'm grateful to the brilliant and generous Deborah Roberts for gifting me with this stunning image for the cover. I'm thankful to Joan Morgan, "the queen of hip-hop feminism," for always asking rich questions and for seeing me and my work in ways that help me to see myself more clearly. I'm indebted to E. Patrick Johnson for writing the foreword, and for modeling what it means to unapologetically embrace one's identity as an artist and scholar in the academy. This play collection would not exist without the wisdom of my long-standing interlocutor and dear friend, Ricardo Bracho, who first suggested it. For decades I've been the beneficiary of his tough love, priceless advice, brilliant dramaturgy, keen wit, and infectious laughter.

Although *Underground*, *Monroe*, and *The Mamalogues* had their first productions in Austin, this play collection truly began in San Francisco, the city where I was raised. My entire family has been integral to my journey as a writer and has always inspired me and supported my work. I must thank my big-hearted cousins, Raymond and Sandra Fontenot, who cared for my son so that I could attend a two-week artist residency. I appreciate my nieces and nephew for always going to great lengths to support their Auntie L. My parents have passed away, but the lessons they taught me continue to influence my work. My late father, Walter Thompson Jr., instilled in me a love for storytelling and performance. He captivated people because his personality was larger than life and so were his tales. My late mother, Herberdine Thompson, is the gentle soul who taught me to read and love books and nurtured me as a writer. My mother is responsible for my first publication in San Francisco's *Sun Reporter*, when I was a mere high school student. It's truly a gift to have a parent who believes in your dreams before you do.

I began "writing shows" with my brother Robert Thompson in the bedroom we shared with our older brother. We were supposed to be asleep in our twin beds. Instead we stayed awake late into the night creating characters and worlds that were bigger, wilder, and more colorful than our neighborhood. I'm forever grateful to Robert, my first writing partner, playmate, confidante, and friend. This play collection is dedicated to him and to our dear siblings, Debra Veley and Guy Thompson. Finally, I must thank my extraordinary son, Femi Makinde, who is my most cherished audience member and greatest blessing. None of my work is possible without his support, patience, and love. May he and his generation use their imaginations to remake this world into a more loving, beautiful, safe, and just place for all.

UNDERGROUND, *MONROE*, AND *THE MAMALOGUES*

UNDERGROUND

When someone asks me about violence, I just find it incredible, because what it means is that the person who's asking that question has absolutely no idea what black people have gone through, what black people have experienced in this country, since the time the first black person was kidnapped from the shores of Africa.

—Angela Davis

PRODUCTION HISTORY

Underground was developed with support from the ScriptWorks Seed Support Fund. *Underground* had its world premiere at The Vortex (Bonnie Cullum, Artistic Director) in Austin, Texas, on March 24, 2017. The production received a ScriptWorks Finer Point grant and funding from the John L. Warfield Center for African and African American Studies at the University of Texas at Austin. Dramaturgy was by Florinda Bryant, scenic design by Ann Marie Gordon, lighting design by Patrick Anthony, costume design by Shannon Mott, sound design by Valerie Johnson and David DeMaris, stage management by Tamara L. Farley, and photography by Errich Petersen. Rudy Ramirez directed the following cast:

Kyle Brown . . . . Marc Pouhé
Mason Dixon . . . . Jeffery Da'Shade Johnson

CHARACTERS

Kyle Brown, a fifty-year-old black man who is as flashy as his off-the-rack three-piece suits and diamond studs. His nickname is "K." He is sly and spirited with a revolutionary entrepreneurial spirit. He is known widely as a protest hustler. He moves and talks fast. His eyes reveal that he's willing to kill. He has stared down the barrel of more than one gun. Raised in the comfort of L.A.'s View Park neighborhood aka "Pill Hill," but has perfected his performance as a "boy from the 'hood."

Mason Nathaniel Dixon, a forty-seven-year-old black lawyer who wears conservative dark Italian two-button suits to court and high-end casual wear on weekends. Once upon a time he went by "Dix," but no longer. He believes in both style and substance. A native of South Central Los Angeles who tries to keep his 'hood upbringing hidden beneath the surface. No jewelry, no Nikes.

SETTING

The present. Mason Dixon's impeccable 1855 brownstone in Albany, New York. It was once a stop on the Underground Railroad. The home has several bedrooms, hardwood floors, exposed brick, a wooden staircase, and high ceilings, with multiple fireplaces throughout. It has been professionally renovated and restored to its prior glory with some new additions, including a modern chef's kitchen with a Sub-Zero fridge and a Viking range. There is a prominent bar area with a collection of decanters and various bottles of fine scotch and bourbon and a wine collection. A brown leather club chair and sofa sit in front of a flat-screen TV and a wooden bookshelf. In the living room a handsome chess set rests on a pedestal in a corner.

The action takes place over one long winter evening.

PLAYWRIGHT'S NOTE

This realist play exists within the absurdity, the surrealism, of the American racial landscape. The pre-show music, the *Underground* mixtape, should be a symphony or soundtrack of contemporary protest music by black artists who rage against the normality of that absurdity. Consider playing the following songs in no particular order during the pre-show and intermission:

The Roots, "How I Got Over"
Billie Holiday, "Strange Fruit"
Stevie Wonder, "You Haven't Done Nothin'"
Kendrick Lamar, "Alright"
Nina Simone, "Backlash Blues"
Nas, "If I Ruled the World"
Marvin Gaye, "What's Going On"
James Brown, "Say It Loud, I'm Black and I'm Proud"
Odetta, "Masters of War"
D'Angelou and the Vanguard, "1000 Deaths"
Harold Melvin and the Blue Notes, "Wake Up Everybody"
Sweet Honey in the Rock, "I'm Going to Get My Baby Out of Jail"
Janelle Monáe, "Hell You Talmbout"
Sam Cooke, "A Change Is Gonna Come"
A Tribe Called Quest, "The Space Program"
2Pac (Tupac Shakur), "Holler If Ya Hear Me"
Tracy Chapman, "Talkin' Bout a Revolution"
Steel Pulse, "Handsworth Revolution"
Gil Scott-Heron, "The Revolution Will Not Be Televised"

PROLOGUE

[*Darkness. The sound of furtive movements and then the sound of a fuse being lit and a ticking clock. The clock ticking increases until it reaches a crescendo. Then silence. Two figures meet in the darkness and begin a quiet huddle. It becomes apparent it's two men meeting in the shadows outside a suburban home. One of them has a small bag.*]

[*Spoken in hurried hushed tones.*]

KYLE: What took you so long?
MASON: Sorry. I had trouble getting away without anyone seeing me.
KYLE: Did anyone follow you here?
MASON: No. I don't think so. I was careful.
KYLE: OK. So you left it? It's done?
MASON: Yeah. It's done.
KYLE: Cool. Listen, you're a part of this now.
MASON: All the way.

[*They engage in an elaborate handshake, hug each other briefly, then stealthily go their separate ways. Darkness falls.*]

ACT 1

[*Evening. Living room of* MASON DIXON*'s home. Loud, incessant knocking at the front door.*]

MASON [*from upstairs*]: Just a minute. I'm coming!

[MASON *bounds down the stairs while removing his tie and unbuttoning his shirt collar. Opens the front door. Surprised. Beat.*]

Kyle?

[KYLE *stands at the door, overdressed in winter clothes—hat, gloves, scarf, and a huge coat. He is dragging a wheeled piece of luggage and carrying a briefcase. He places the briefcase carefully on the floor and throws his arms open wide.*]

KYLE: In the flesh, nigga!
MASON: I didn't know you were out here.
KYLE [*with snow falling from his jacket all over* MASON*'s hardwood floors*]: Yeah, well here I am doing a little business in the city and—
MASON [*somewhat annoyed by the snow on the floor*]: Is that right? Um. Come in, man. It's been awhile.
KYLE: Long while. Wait. [*Taking off coat, hat, scarf, and gloves*] Let me get a look at you! [*Giving* MASON *a bear hug*] Wow, it's really good to see you, brotha!

[KYLE *hugs* MASON *again.* MASON *stiffens at the emotional display and backs away awkwardly.*]

MASON: Yeah. Well, let me take your coat.

[MASON *proceeds to the closet with* KYLE*'s coat, grabs a broom, and sweeps the snow outside while* KYLE *watches.*]

KYLE: Sorry about that.
MASON [*putting away the broom*]: Don't worry about it.
KYLE: Thanks!
MASON: So, what kind of business brings you all the way up here?
KYLE: We'll get to all that in a minute. Let me warm up! Damn! Isn't it supposed to be spring?
MASON: Not yet.

KYLE: I see. It's cold as fuck! I can't believe all that snow out there!

[KYLE *looks out the window.*]

MASON: I'm used to it.

KYLE: Good to see you, bruh. I said to myself, "I can't be this close and not hit up my boy!" I'm not gonna let no little snowstorm stand in my way. You ain't nothing but a hop, skip, and a jump from the city.

MASON: More like a hop, skip, and a two-and-a-half hour train ride.

KYLE: Two-and-a-half hours? Hmm. Well, the time flew by. [*Riffling through his bags*] I made a few calls and the next thing I know they're announcing Albany, Schenectady—I rode on the side with a view of the Hudson River.

MASON: Yes, it's a nice ride. Very relaxing.

KYLE: Not sure how relaxing it was. Quite a police presence at the stations. I haven't seen them flexing like that in years.

MASON: They're still on the lookout for the leader of that radical group.

KYLE: Yeah. The Feds are kinda shook.

MASON: I guess so. [*Clearing some newspapers off the sofa*] Have a seat.

KYLE: Thanks. [*Sitting down and placing his briefcase on his lap*] The ride was cool. I could chill, think, and make a few calls. I called you at the office, but your secretary said you were working upstate today.

MASON: Sometimes it's easier to get writing done outside of the office.

KYLE: I hear you. I guess you can say I'm doing the same. Handling my business on the road. By the way, I have a little something I really need to rap with you about.

[KYLE *taps on the briefcase.*]

MASON: Slow down, K. You just arrived. I haven't seen you in what?

KYLE: Seven, eight years.

MASON: Wow. Forgive my manners. Can I get you a drink? Something to warm you up. Rum and Coke, right?

KYLE: I'm a Jack man now. Jack and Coke, if you got it. And some ice.

MASON: Hey, sorry I couldn't make it to that protest the last time I was in L.A. The firm had me locked down in depositions. That police brutality case, right?

KYLE: Yeah. Another one. You missed it! I was flowing up there. Sometimes I feel like the spirits of past warriors are speaking through me.

MASON: You got good folks writing for you.

KYLE: What can I say. I know how to spot talent. Now, your writing was phenomenal. After all these years, I still miss your pen.

MASON: Mightier than the sword.

KYLE: Sometimes. It all depends on the kind of battle you're waging.

MASON: You're getting some good coverage with those words. For a minute, it seemed like whenever I watched the news—there you are on the screen.

KYLE: Can you blame me if folks love a handsome face and a loud mouth?

MASON: Seriously though. Bringing the Crips and Bloods together was no small feat. You deserve props for that. The press was all over you for that one.

KYLE: Thanks, but I don't do anything for the coverage. [*Raising his glass*] I do it all for the culture.

MASON: I heard you got Bad Boy and Death Row Records to come to the table back in the day?

KYLE [*surprised*]: Not too many folks know about that.

MASON: Now I wish I could have been at that meeting!

KYLE: The front seats are only for the paying customers. Besides it didn't go too well.

MASON: Well, I guess even you can't win them all.

KYLE: Yes, but a warrior keeps on trying. [*Beat*] You have no idea how hard it is to get folks to negotiate. Sometimes I wonder if it's even worth it.

MASON: Beats the alternative. The firm always tries to settle instead of going to court. We save our resources for those times when we have to go to war. Besides, your high-profile negotiations keep you in the limelight.

KYLE: Off camera moves in the dark are often more important than the acts carried out in the light.

MASON: Well, the next time I'm back in L.A. I'll make sure to come through and—

KYLE: Hey, don't sweat it, Dix. You're a busy and important man. Sometimes you've got to bring the mountain to Mohammed. Hope you don't mind the surprise. You said if I'm ever in town I should fall through.

MASON: Yes, of course. [*Handing him a highball glass*] Let me know if that works. So, what exactly brings you—

KYLE: Just what I need! [*Watching* MASON *make another cocktail*] I remember you use to like them bitch-ass drinks. What you got there?

MASON: Scotch. Neat.

KYLE: Well damn! Somebody grew up! You all man now. [*Attempting a toast*] To Mason Nathaniel Dixon. To Dix!

MASON [*pulling back his glass*]: Just Mason.

KYLE: OK, OK. So, here's to . . . reunions, just Mason!

[*The pair awkwardly toast again.*]

Whoa!! Damn! [*Coughing a little. Whispering raspily*] That's strong.

MASON: Need more ice?

KYLE [*coughing again*]: Naw, I'm good. Chilling with Dix! My little brother from another mother. [*Taking another sip*] Damn! Now that's a drink!

MASON: You sure you don't need some more ice?

KYLE: Naw, I'm cool. [*Tentatively taking another sip*] You can hit me with a little more of that Coke though.

MASON: I got you.

KYLE: Thanks! [*Beat*] I'm not sweating you but it would really help me out if—

MASON [*freshening his drink*]: Remind me again, how long you going to be on the East Coast?

KYLE: I didn't say. It all depends on how my meetings go. Things are kinda open-ended right now.

MASON [*handing him the new drink*]: Open-ended?

KYLE: Thanks.

MASON: You were saying things are open-ended?

KYLE: Yeah, but if it all goes well I can get out of here and back to civilization. No offense! [*Looking out a different window this time*] How you stay up here in all this damn snow?

MASON: You get used to it. I'm good.

KYLE: We all good. Now we weren't good when we ran the yard though! [*Laughing*] We was some bad mothafuckas back in the day.

MASON [*sober*]: Well these days I only run around the park.

KYLE [*leaving the window*]: Oh yeah? Better be glad the cops don't think you're running away from something. Might find yourself on the wrong side of a barrel and a man in blue.

MASON: I'll take my chances. So, what time do you need to get back down to the city? You're staying up here until—?

KYLE: Tomorrow. I don't want to put you out.

MASON: Hey, it's not a problem but I can't hang too tough. I'm swamped. I came up here to write. I've got this brief to finish by morning so—

KYLE: Handle yours, brotha. I ain't trying to get all in your mix. I ain't here to get in the way. I can always get me a room downtown.

MASON: I didn't say anything about—

KYLE: Listen, if it's an issue—

MASON: I said you can stay. Chill.

KYLE: Cool. I really appreciate it, little brother. [*Grabbing his phone*] Let me check on something. My phone kept fucking up on the train. Couldn't get a damn signal half the time. Now my battery is dying. Can I plug it in somewhere?

MASON: Of course. Go ahead and use that outlet over there.

KYLE: These phones always got me on the run. Gotta back it up, gotta charge it, and then you gotta get a new one every year. They're worse than bitches!

MASON [*cringing*]: Right.

[KYLE *plugs in his phone, then takes note of the art on the wall.*]

KYLE: Cool painting. Where'd you get it from?

MASON: It was a gift from the other partners at the firm. I was lead on a copyright infringement case a few years back. My client received a pretty nice settlement.

KYLE: You made now, brotha! I'm not surprised. You were always a tough little dude. Even when you were a sophomore you had swag. Writing like Baldwin, with the heart of Che, Fred Hampton, Malcolm—

MASON: OK, OK. Man, slow down.

[MASON*'s phone rings; he looks at it, recognizes the number, but allows it to go to voice mail.*]

[*Sending a text*] You want another drink, K?

KYLE: Don't mind if I do, but go light on that Jack.

MASON [*making the drink*]: Got it. You want something to eat? I was about to throw together a salad. I picked up some pasta from an Italian spot around the corner. They're pretty tight.

KYLE: I don't want to put you out. I showed up out of nowhere and now I got you up here being Martha Stewart.

MASON: Hey man, it's cool. It's just a salad. I've got plenty of food. I need to eat something anyway before I get down to work.

KYLE: You sure?

MASON: Not a problem.

KYLE: Well if you're going to throw something together anyway I guess I could go ahead and eat too. You said pasta?

MASON: Baked ziti.

KYLE: Any meat in it or have you gone vegan on me?

MASON [*preparing the salad*]: Turkey meatballs.

KYLE: If you eating it then it can't be but so bad.

MASON: I'm glad you approve.

KYLE: Is that kale? Damn you gone super healthy on my ass.

MASON: I don't know about you but I'm trying to live.

KYLE: Ain't we all? Hey, I can make my own plate, bro. Just show me where the—

MASON: Hey, it's not a problem. Relax. Just fall back a little.

[MASON *heads to the kitchen for plates and utensils and begins preparing the food.*]

KYLE: Thanks. That mess they were serving in the dining car didn't look too good. [*Taking off his shoes and loosening his tie*] Dix and K, shit! Back together again. We are still sharp as a tack. Bad as hell if I do say so my damn self!

MASON: Where did you get those?

KYLE [*holding up one of his shiny shoes*]: Straight from motherfuckin' Paris, nigga! I caught me a nice shine at Penn Station from this older cat. Said he use to run with the Young Lords back in the day. Imagine that. This sista I was kicking it with in Baltimore picked them up for me. [*Pointing to a pair of shoes by the door, where he places his own shoes*] Where did you get these kicks?

MASON: Maybe Prada—I can't recall.

KYLE: Straight out of Prada, huh? [*Looking at* MASON*'s bookshelves*] I see you, player. I love it. I remember when you were straight out of Compton!

MASON: Well, I'm still the same, man.

KYLE: I bet.

MASON: Compton born and bred—just making my way in a new world.

KYLE: But we can never stray too far away from our roots. It's time for a return to old school. What did we use to say? "King and Malcolm changed the world clad in the armor of suits and ties."

MASON: I don't remember saying all that.

KYLE: Come on! We studied that shit. And the Panthers too! Black leather, berets, and 'fros. Iconic! We were fly cool ourselves back in the day. Remember my leather Malcolm X medallion and that Kufi you use to rock at those divestment rallies? The honeys were all ready to—

MASON: Like I said, I don't remember all that. Besides, that's all ancient history now. I'm a one-woman man now. [*Handing him a plate*] Here you go. I hope you like it.

KYLE: Thanks, brotha! [*Talking while he eats*] I'm just saying. Every era has its look, but these young brothers now? These knuckleheads be running around in sagging pants, big ass T-shirts, and sneakers. Yea, I'm cool with hip-hop, but I don't understand why a grown-ass man is rocking clothes like he's a rapper and shit. I'm like come on, man! Everybody knows you're an accountant.

MASON: It doesn't bother me. They got their thing. Back then fifty- and sixty-year-old dudes weren't feeling our little outfits either.

KYLE: Little outfits? I don't know about you but I was clean! From the looks of things you still ain't above all that now. I'm just talking about us making history, bruh.

[KYLE *finishes his drink in one gulp.*]

MASON: History?

KYLE: Yes. We made shit happen! Think about it. Back in the eighties did you ever think we'd live to see Mandela freed?

MASON: Not really, no. I can't say I did.

KYLE: He passed away peacefully in his bed at ninety-five years old. A legend. We helped make that happen. We made our mark with the divestment movement and on the world stage. I'm proud of what we did to help end apartheid.

MASON: That's a little over the top—even for you, K.

KYLE: What are you talking about? We cut our teeth trying to—

MASON: Come on! I was there. We were just a bunch of college kids.

KYLE: Naw! We were young revolutionaries. That was our abolitionist struggle, our anti-lynching crusade, our civil rights movement, our Black Power movement!

MASON: So you gonna take it there? Come on!

KYLE: We shut that university down for two weeks!

MASON: More like a few days.

KYLE: What? Come on!

MASON: And it was a classic university sit-in. Nothing more.

KYLE: Oh yeah? It was pretty serious according to my folks. Remember that fit my daddy threw?

MASON: Yeah. [*Speaking as* KYLE*'s father*] "Young man, your mother and I did not send you to school to start a riot! Have you lost your mind?"

KYLE [*as young* KYLE]: "But Daddy!"

MASON: "That sit-in mess is over—"

KYLE: "But Daddy!"

MASON: "Do you want those cops to kill you? They are perfectly happy to oblige your death wish."

KYLE: "But Daddy!"

MASON AND KYLE: "You are not in college to play out some Fidel Castro fantasy!"

KYLE [*laughing*]: What did I expect from the judge?

MASON [*as* KYLE*'s father*]: "Son, if you continue I will no longer pay for your tuition and your automobile—"

KYLE: He could be an assassin. A real cold dude!

MASON: "Your car will be repossessed by me and stored here at the house until further notice."

KYLE: Not the Civic! I can't believe he threated to take the revolutionary pimpmobile! Pops did not play!

MASON: But you wouldn't back down.

KYLE: Keeping it real? That was the first time I really stood up to him. That protest meant more to me than school—

MASON: —even more important than the sistas?

KYLE: Yeah, if you can believe it. You were pretty dedicated to the cause back then too. Did they ever find out who bombed that building on campus?

MASON: So, it was classified a bombing? I thought an experiment went wrong in one of the labs.

KYLE: Whatever it was "classified as" it certainly frayed some nerves. After that incident at the registrar's office the president was really shook. He moved off campus for a while, talking some garbage about needing the residence retrofitted to survive an earthquake.

MASON: Yeah. That I remember.

KYLE: Didn't you get called in about that?

MASON: About what? The explosion? [*Slowly. Unsure about how much to recount of the story*] No. Well, the Dean wanted to bring me in . . .

KYLE: Uh huh.

MASON: But your pops . . . um. He saved the day. He got the university to stand down.

KYLE: That's right. With your whole life ahead of you and your back against the wall—here come da judge to clear the way for a brave young soldier.

MASON: Your dad said the university only listened because they didn't want to piss off a generous donor.

KYLE: Daddy always knew how to use that green to back up his mouth.

MASON: Your father is a great man.

KYLE: Sure he is, as long as you don't disappoint him! [*Beat*] So after all that died down you became the anti-apartheid poster boy, right? The administration could never touch you. Didn't that get you into more draws than—

MASON: Wow, man! You're always talking about women.

KYLE: Yes, sir. The black female in particular. Best topic in the world.

MASON: Some things never change.

KYLE: Females are one of the true hazards of my profession.

MASON: Is that right? Well, I don't know anything about "females" but I know a few things about women.

KYLE: Forgive my language. You know I'm just talking shit. What can I say, I'm just old school. Don't you understand it's hard out here for an old freedom fighter? Have a heart, brotha.

MASON: Of course. I've got plenty of love for an old freedom fighter. Especially one who's never been imprisoned, shot, or worse. So, does that make you a fake revolutionary? Or just lucky?

KYLE: Lucky? I know you ain't up here talking about luck. You made it out of south central L.A. with a fancy law degree. I'm not the one who—

MASON: That wasn't about luck for me. After all, my folks didn't lay everything out on a silver platter for me.

KYLE: Maybe it looked that way from the outside but—

MASON: I wouldn't know anything about that. My pops died owing me money.

KYLE: There is skill and talent involved in this hustle, best believe.

MASON: I know all about skill and talent. I know about sacrifice and risk too.

KYLE: Seems like you're all good now. [*Walking around the house picking up and appraising items*] A spot upstate, a little something in the city. No, you ain't exactly hard up for cash these days. It's a far cry from when we were in school. And you're a wonderful host. Thanks for the grub.

MASON: Don't mention it.

KYLE: Now where should I put this?

MASON: I'll take that.

[MASON *takes the dishes out while* KYLE *begins to look at his phone and type a quick text.* MASON *yells from the kitchen.*]

Yeah, I'm doing OK. What about you? [*Returning*] So really, how's the revolutionary game? You don't seem to be struggling either.

KYLE: No complaints, brotha. I'm fine as wine. You finished with the dishes that fast?

MASON: No, I'll tackle that mess in the morning.

KYLE: You sure? I can still bust some suds.

MASON: Don't worry about it. You're my guest.

KYLE: If you're sure, let me tell you why I came—

MASON: Wait! I'm really slipping. How is the judge's health these days? When I heard about the stroke I called your mom and sent flowers. I'm sorry. I meant to reach out to you too, but time just—

KYLE: Don't worry about it. You couldn't have reached me anyway. I was out of the country at the time—working with some comrades in

Cuba. Pops is much better now. Thanks for asking. You should see him walking around with this elaborate cane with a brass handle. He'd pass out if I told him he looked like a pimp with that thing. It's quiet around the house now. He never regained his ability to speak. I'm just glad we buried the hatchet a few years before all that jumped off.

MASON: That's a relief. It's important to make peace.

KYLE: Yes, if you can.

MASON: Please give him my regards when you see him.

KYLE: Yeah. Will do. So how's your moms doing? Such a sweet woman.

MASON: Moms is fine. Still working. Volunteering at church. The usual.

KYLE: Of course she is. She ain't sweating you about giving her some grandkids?

MASON: No, Dee gave her three fat grandbabies in rapid succession. Twin girls and a boy so I'm off the hook for life. What about you? With your antics I thought you'd have enough kids to field a basketball team by now.

KYLE: The community is my family and I'm a devoted father.

MASON: I bet. Well, I need to get back to—

KYLE: You still smoke?

MASON: Do I need to remind you that I'm an officer of the court?

KYLE: Motherfucka, please! You know how many coke-head lawyers I know that get high on the regular?

MASON: Tell me you don't do blow—

KYLE: What I look like? Some kinda dopehead? Come on, man.

MASON: Hey, sorry. It's been a minute. I don't know what you're into now—

KYLE: Listen, I just hit a little weed every now and then. Strictly for medicinal purposes of course. [*Winking*] Glaucoma.

MASON: Right.

KYLE: So, you cool if I twist one up?

MASON: I've never been able to stop you from doing what you want. Go ahead, do your thing.

[*During the next exchange,* KYLE *engages in an elaborate production of rolling a fat joint or two while* MASON *observes.* KYLE *lights the joint, takes a puff and offers some to* MASON.]

KYLE: Always, player. Always got to do my thing.

MASON: So are the rumors true about what you've been getting into?

KYLE: What? Rumors? Who you been talking to? Benny? He's a fool. I wouldn't listen to him to save my life. There's always talk. What did you hear?

MASON: The word in the blogs and on the street is that there's a TV show in the works. You're on your way to being a star!

KYLE: Oh that. Yeah. Maybe so. That's actually one of the things I want to rap with you about.

MASON: I should have known that's where you were headed. Your spot on that Panther documentary was tight. The camera loves you.

KYLE: Look at this face? Why wouldn't it? Besides, TV is just one platform to advance our agenda.

MASON: It seems a black man can have it all: the revolution and a steady paycheck too? I guess you can't ask for more than that. Jesse had a show. Sharpton had a show. I guess you all get one eventually.

KYLE: Why you clownin' a brotha?

MASON: Oh, no conk or rhyming?

KYLE: You really got jokes tonight. Just make sure your ass tunes in to my conk-free revolutionary rap television.

MASON: I'll make it a habit. With your gifts I do believe a talk show is something you could excel at. I'd watch it!

KYLE: This ain't about me though. It's a means to an end. If we can get to folks where they are—through TV and social media—then I have an opportunity to push some real change. The money I make helps fund my organization's "riskier" projects.

MASON: Now I can respect that.

KYLE: I'm glad I can get your approval. What I could really use is your professional expertise. It'd be cool to have you in on this hustle just like old times.

MASON: Is that right? I'm done writing speeches.

KYLE: No, not that, although that would be cool. Actually, I got some complications that might get in the way, but if the offer comes through I'd appreciate it if you would review the contract?

MASON: I don't do that kind of law. I generally handle property—intellectual property, but I can put you onto—

KYLE: Naw, brotha. I ain't messing with nobody else. It's gotta be you. I need somebody I can trust. Somebody I got history with, you hear me?

MASON [*after a beat*]: Let's just see what happens. I wish you luck with all that, K.

KYLE: Appreciate it. Gotta dream big, for my people. I know you're feeling some kinda way about being involved but you know it would be dope to have you on as a regular guest.

MASON: Come again?

KYLE: As a talking head. An expert! A commenta-tor! K & Dix back together for real.

MASON: Me? As TV pundit? You're trippin'. Naw, I'm going to have to pass on that. Thanks though.

KYLE: Come on. This producer told me I need some prominent names attached to help me pitch the show. I figure that I need me an upstanding Negro from the black professional class.

MASON: You won't have any problems booking prominent Negroes. I'm sure you'll have an entire green room full of black public intellectuals ready to share their plan to save our people and promote their brand.

KYLE: Hey! You can't knock the hustle. I just want the right folks on the screen speaking truth to power. We could really use some of your expertise. You can school my audience on avoiding, hmm, how should I put it, "legal complications," while fomenting revolution?

MASON: Like the kind of trouble these New Movement folks got themselves caught up in? They're going to need more than competent legal representation. Seriously. I can't believe those fools are going around bombing shit!

KYLE: Why not? It's the American way. This country was built on massacres, lynching, genocide, riots, and beatings. The national pastime is war, then baseball.

MASON: They've been lucky so far—

KYLE: Or strategic.

MASON: Nobody has been hurt but—

KYLE: Their targets have been wisely selected: government buildings, Confederate statues—

MASON: Hitting at the heart of the empire.

KYLE: All fair targets in guerrilla warfare.

MASON: You think so? Look K, there are real consequences to this. I don't want any parts of it. I don't want to provide advice or even want to speak on domestic terrorism—

KYLE: Domestic terrorism?

MASON: —on yours or anyone else's television program. Besides, I've got a morality clause in my contract.

KYLE: Wow! You really got a problem with what they're doing?

MASON: Yes, I do. I'm not trying to throw away my career or the life I've put together.

KYLE: Can't upset old massa huh?

MASON: You sure you want the white man all up in your mix?

KYLE: He's always in the mix though, right? We both know that. Come on! You gonna turn an old friend down just like that?

MASON: I'll review *your* contract but after that I'm out.

KYLE: Come on. We always worked well together. I don't see why we need to end it there. Just let me hit you up with some possible topics.

MASON: You still can't take no for an answer, huh?

KYLE: The revolution still needs you.

MASON: It seems to be going pretty well without me! I'm good.

KYLE: Cool, cool. I hear you.

MASON [*annoyed*]: Like I said I need to get back to work. The sheets in the guest room are clean and there should be some space in the closet to hang your . . . suits.

KYLE: Cool. Thanks.

MASON: Don't sweat it.

KYLE: You gonna be able to get all this work done with me at the pad?

MASON: Don't worry about it.

KYLE: I appreciate the hospitality.

MASON: Don't mention it, K. Let me get you some towels. [*Reaching for his luggage*] Let me take this [*trying to grab the briefcase*] upstairs and put it with your other—

KYLE: No! [*Softening*] Thanks. I'll handle this.

[KYLE *picks up the briefcase and puts it by his side.*]

I need to keep that close by. I might need something out of it.

MASON: All right.

[*Taken aback. Runs upstairs.*]

KYLE: Don't rush, brotha.

[*Checks his cell phone, then looks through his briefcase, then sends a text. While* MASON *is upstairs,* KYLE *moves through the room casually riffling through* MASON*'s things.*]

We're too old to be rushing around. I like to take my time and chill. I flow like molasses. Folks have heart attacks running crazy. That won't happen to me. When I get off the road a bit I like to relax. [*Looking outside the window, then resuming his snooping*] That snow still hasn't stopped and those flakes look big as hell. I guess it's cool if you like to go skiing and shit like that. I never got the why folks find that fun. Sliding down a hill on two pieces of wood was never my cup of tea. I guess white folks need to invent shit to be excited about. Hey, I think it's coming down harder.

MASON [*from upstairs*]: I've been so wrapped up with work, I haven't checked the forecast. Probably a Nor'easter coming.

KYLE: What?

[KYLE *continues looking through* MASON*'s mail, laptop, and drawers.*]

MASON [*from upstairs*]: A Nor'easter. A big snowstorm that dumps massive amounts of snow on the Northeast.

KYLE: Damn! I hope not. I cannot get trapped up here. I got things to do. Hey, if you don't mind I'm gonna make myself another drink. Maybe that will take the chill out of my bones.

MASON [*from upstairs*]: Go ahead! Make yourself at home.

KYLE: Thanks!

[KYLE *hears footsteps coming and begins to make the drink.*]

You want another one?

[MASON *returns from upstairs with a pile of dirty laundry and tosses it in the mudroom off the kitchen.*]

MASON: I'm gonna have to pass. I need a clear head for work. I left some towels on the bed and put your suitcase in the closet.

KYLE: Cool. You're a true prince.

MASON: You're killing me, man.
KYLE: Great library you've got here.
MASON: Thanks.
KYLE [*browsing the bookshelf*]: Baldwin, Hughes, Sanchez, Morrison, Wilson, Baraka, Walker. All the greats. You always loved great writing.
MASON: It's good for the soul. Why don't you go on upstairs and get settled—
KYLE: Not just yet. I'm good right here for now. So—

[KYLE*'s cell phone rings but* KYLE *ignores it.*]

MASON: You gonna get that?
KYLE: No, I'm cool.
MASON: OK. Well, like I said I have a brief that—
KYLE: Brotha, go ahead and write your shit. I'm cool.

[KYLE *picks up the phone and sends a quick text.*]

It won't bother me, but when you take a break let me holla at you a little bit about this situation.
MASON: Sure but I need to put this to rest before—

[MASON *opens his laptop and starts typing. The phone rings again.*]

KYLE: Damn! Excuse me. They won't let up. I gotta take this. [*Into phone*] Hello, K. Brown here. [*Pause. Stepping as far away from* MASON *as possible*] Yeah. No, I haven't. He seems cool. I got it with me. Don't worry, I have it with me. [*Looking out the window again*] Let me talk with him—I'll find out and get back at you. Sure. [*Beat*] I can't right now. [*Beat*] Then tell them to wait!

[KYLE *hangs up the phone.*]

MASON [*barely looking up from the laptop*]: Everything OK?
KYLE: Yeah, I'm cool, but like I said I do need to rap with you about—
MASON: I can't now—later, OK? [*Beat*] I'm sorry. I just need to stay focused.

[MASON *resumes working on his laptop.*]

KYLE: Right. OK, Dix. By all means keep your head straight. Do your thing, man.

[KYLE *puts on a pair of wireless headphones, then swipes through his phone. He begins to sing, dance, and snap his fingers.*]

"Brother, brother. There's far too many of you dying." Nothing like an old school jam! Oh man. Hell, yeah. That's my song!

[*Marvin Gaye's "What's Going On" or "Inner City Blues (Make Me Wanna Holler)" plays as if coming from* KYLE*'s headphones.*]

[MASON *receives a text. He reads it and jumps up to turn on the television.*]

MASON: K! K! Kyle!

[KYLE *takes off his headphones.*]

Man, check this out!

[MASON *turns up the volume.*]

KYLE: It's really jumping off now.

[*News anchorwoman voice-over while* KYLE *begins rolling another joint.* MASON *sits in rapt attention.*]

VOICE-OVER: What began in California just a few weeks ago has begun to spread east. Police and federal agents continue to look for suspects in connection with several bombings at government buildings in the west.

MASON: They're on the hunt!

VOICE-OVER: Sources close to the investigation say that those incidents are connected to the recent explosions in the New York metropolitan area.

[KYLE *and* MASON *both begin sending quick texts.*]

Officials have declined to release the names of the suspects, citing national security concerns.

KYLE: National security? Right! These motherfuckers always want to raise the stakes. I can't believe—

MASON: Sshh!

VOICE-OVER: Our source also revealed that the focus is on apprehending the leader or leaders behind New Movement, a radical group similar to the Black Panthers. Their tactics include the use of deadly force and authorities believe—

MASON [*turning off the news*]: Whoa.

KYLE: Deadly force?

MASON: Yeah.

KYLE: Tracking him like a runaway slave. Damn. They can't snuff out a movement once it has ignited the imagination of the people.

MASON: What are you talking about? This isn't a game. I can't believe these folks are out here on some terrorism shit.

KYLE: It's the resistance. This is what it looks like to fight back.

MASON: I understand that, but when you're talking about violence, loss of life—

KYLE: Loss of life? As far as I know, New Movement hasn't killed anybody—

MASON: Yet!

KYLE: Come on! The media always gotta take it there when our folks are involved. The propaganda machine is the real deadly force.

MASON: Wait. This is not just sensational journalism. They are out here bombing shit, man.

KYLE: Things. Not people. Statues of long dead white men can't die again. Empty buildings. Those armed militia white boys had a national park occupied for months and they were called peaceful protesters.

MASON: Come on, K. They are setting off explosives!

KYLE: They're also igniting imaginations. New Movement ain't no joke. Insurrection! It's about time. They can't continue with this injustice and expect to ride for free throughout eternity.

MASON: Negotiating for a payday with a finger on the trigger? That's terrorism.

KYLE: That's revolution.

MASON: They're tripping for real, man. This won't end well.

[*Flashback to 1988. The offices of the Black Student Union.* KYLE *is playing solitaire.*]

KYLE: Hey Prep! What are you doing up here?

MASON: I just wanted to see what was up. I heard you at the rally.

KYLE: You got some of that soul food, huh?

MASON: Yeah. I liked what you said.

KYLE: Apartheid must fall, young brother. We need divestment now!

MASON: That's why I'm here. I want to join. I want to help.

KYLE: You wanna join us, huh? Weren't you just pledging Alpha?

MASON: Kappa. But it wasn't for me.

KYLE: Is that right? [*Doing some fraternity step show moves*] Too much stepping and not going nowhere, huh?

MASON: Something like that.

KYLE: Well, man, I don't want there to be any confusion. This ain't nothing like a frat, young blood. We are the BSA. We are men and women of purpose who are about the business of our people. I'm Chairman of the Black Student Association. The only radical organization on this entire campus. No step shows, no line brothers, no parties, no sorority girls (well, maybe a few), but no bullshitting. This is about overturning the status quo! This is about changing the world. And remember this, if you don't remember anything else: ain't no quitting allowed.

MASON: I understand.

KYLE [*looks him over*]: Come by Friday night. The crew gotta check you out and see how you think. You up for some Bid Whist and Spades?

MASON: Yeah, I'll come by but . . . I don't play cards.

KYLE: All right, you slap some bones? [*Registering the uneasy look on* MASON*'s face*] No bones either?

MASON: Naw, I can't play dominoes but I can learn.

KYLE: What do you play?

MASON [*beat, then speaking low*]: Chess.

KYLE: What? Don't be shy. Speak up!

MASON [*louder*]: Chess. I play chess.

KYLE: Chess! You a real white boy, ain't you?

MASON: Excuse me?

KYLE: I'm just fucking with you. I dig chess. That's a cool game.

MASON [*relieved*]: My uncle taught me back in the day. He learned while he was doing a bid in San Quentin.

KYLE [*gesturing toward the chess set in the corner*]: San Quentin?

MASON: Yeah.

KYLE: I grew up playing chess at the crib. My father calls it the ultimate game of strategy. You ever use a timer? It raises the stakes.

MASON: No, but I'm game.
KYLE: You want to be white?
MASON: What?
KYLE: Your pieces? You want white?
MASON: Black.
KYLE: I'm usually black, but I'll let you have it this time.
MASON: Thanks.
KYLE: Just remember: "Power concedes nothing without demand. It never has—
MASON AND KYLE [*in unison*]: —it never will."
KYLE: The youngster does know a few things. Your move!

[*Hits timer.*]

Your uncle there when George Jackson was locked up?
MASON: No, he did his bid later.
KYLE: I've seen you around. You got a nice little rep from that column you write for the paper.
MASON: I just write what's on my mind. I think divestment from South Africa is the most important issue our people are facing globally.
KYLE: You don't say. That editorial about the ANC was on point. Folks have taken notice.
MASON: Thanks. I write about local issues too.
KYLE: Yeah. Your piece on the faculty was nice.
MASON: There is only one black professor in the English department and he doesn't even have tenure.
KYLE: Nice move. [*Studying the board*] What else you feel passionate about?
MASON: The cost of tuition. It's so high that I've got to work twenty hours a week, plus take out loans. My mom can't help me pay. I live at home to help her out. Things are kinda—
KYLE: Hard knock right? Well, money ain't everything. Trust me. Better for folks to owe you than for you to owe them. If you owe them?

[*Makes chess move. Hits timer.*]

They own you. Don't let nobody get you caught up chasing that dough.
MASON: That's easy to say when you've got it. When you don't . . .

[*Makes a dramatic move on the chess board. Hits timer.*]

KYLE: Damn. Sweet move. I like how you think.

MASON: Thanks! The timer is throwing me off a little but I'll get the hang of it.

[*Hits timer.*]

You're a senior, right?

KYLE: Senior—well a fifth-year senior.

MASON: It's cool that you could afford an extra year.

KYLE: Well, the parents will keep paying as long as I'm staying out of trouble. If they only knew. Yeah, well I decided to stick around an extra year to make sure the organization is on solid ground. It's a critical year for us. The BSA has many projects—on campus, and in the community, especially in the jails and prisons. We have ties to others nationally too. Some of our programs are basic and others are a bit more complex. A few of them are . . . risky.

[*Hits timer.*]

MASON: I understand. That's why I'm here. I'm not worried about danger. At the rally you said that time is of the essence. I'm ready. I agree that if we don't act now—

[*Hits timer.*]

KYLE: Slow down, young blood. I can see that you're eager. The issue is not your willingness but your trustworthiness.

[*Hits timer.*]

MASON: I'm a man of my word. Honor and integrity are everything.

[*Hits timer.*]

KYLE: What would your former line brothers say about that?

MASON: I'll recruit them to join the fight too.

KYLE: OK. Persuasive, deliberate, strategic, and brave too. I'm liking how you think, Dix!

MASON: Thanks, Kyle.

KYLE: Call me K.

MASON: All right, K.

KYLE: So, you claim you're trustworthy but are you hard?
MASON: Hard?
KYLE: Yeah! Hard? Rugged? Badass? Are you tough enough to stand the pressure?

[*Hits timer.*]

If so, maybe someday you'll be the BSA chair.
MASON [*looking* KYLE *in the eye and making a move without looking at the board*]: Just watch me.

[*Hits timer.*]

KYLE: Nobody really knows what they are made of until they are face-to-face with the devil himself.

[*Hits timer and stares at* MASON *long and hard.*]

MASON [*making a measured, decisive move and hitting the timer*]: Queen takes pawn! You thought you had—
KYLE [*making a swift and commanding move*]: Checkmate! There it is. Good game, though.

[*Pause.* KYLE *starts clearing the board.*]

I like you, Dix. I want you to help me with a little errand later. Meet me here tonight at midnight.
MASON: Midnight?
KYLE: That's right. Come alone. Don't be late.
MASON [*clearing pieces off the board*]: You can count on me.

[*Back to the present. Several hours have passed. They're both drunk now and listening to music. Bob Marley's "Get Up Stand Up" is ending.*]

KYLE: You pressed send on that joint like, "Thank you, Massa, for letting me free!"

[KYLE *laughs.*]

MASON: Hey! I ain't nobody's slave but [*laughing*] I can't lie. I'm relieved to be done with that shit though.

[MASON *continually sips his drink and places records on his very expensive turntable with the care of a neurosurgeon operating on an infant.*]

KYLE: Another ironclad contract courtesy of Mason N. Dixon.

MASON: Just doing what I do.

KYLE [*nodding his head to the crackling sound of the stereo needle on wax*]: Ain't nothing like the sound of vinyl, Dix. That's soul food.

[*Parliament-Funkadelic's "One Nation Under a Groove" begins to play.*]

MASON: You remember this?

KYLE [*singing*]: "The funk, the whole funk, and nothing but the funk! You can't stop us now!"

MASON AND KYLE [*singing in unison and busting a few dance steps*]: "One nation under a groove. Getting down just for the funk of it. One nation and we're on the move. Nothing can stop us now!"

KYLE [*begins dancing*]: That's what folks need. The funk! That will lead us out of this wilderness in America.

MASON: Come on, man! It's a cycle. No matter what is happening now, things have changed. Substantially. Don't forget our last president was a brotha!

KYLE [*looking for more music in the stacks*]: Was *is* was. Besides, his ass wasn't my brotha. That dude was way too accommodationist for me. That's the problem with polite Negroes. They're always trying to be acceptable. Always worried about being respectable. Always worried about the optics. Too worried about scaring white folks.

MASON: I know, but—

KYLE: But what? He shoulda been swingin' for the fences when he had the chance! The minute he got in office he should have pushed for everything we deserve. You bourgie Negroes can have him. Always talking down to black folk—Talking about black men not knowing how to be fathers and telling folk to "check your kids' homework" like that's news. Black folk don't need all his "pull yourself up by your bootstraps" garbage!

MASON: Damn! Calm down, Cornel West! Come on! He was just saying what we've all heard brothers say at the barbershop for years.

KYLE: It's fine and good when he's addressing the Negro, but the talented tenth got real salty when he started clowning folks at Morehouse. [*Imitating President Obama*] "Work hard! Stop complaining! Do your best! The world doesn't owe you anything." Them Negroes were up in arms!

MASON: That was straight crazy!

[MASON *puts on an old hip-hop song—Nas, "If I Ruled the World."*]

KYLE: None of that matters now. We are where we are. Our people are at the mercy of a madman. The time is now, Dix. You can't be happy with the way things are for our young people. Ain't nobody hiring them, schools ain't teaching them their history let alone what they need to know to survive. Shit, we were fighting for our lives with him in office. What the hell you expect us to do now? Play nice and wait for the next executive order? This fool might reinstate slavery at this rate.

MASON: I'm not blind! I know these are dire times, but we can't allow it to make us lose ourselves.

KYLE: Dire times? Dire times? They are setting us on the road to annihilation. Not only are they closing off the borders but they're locking us up with them. For what? What's their ultimate plan? Our schools are prisons with armed police roaming the halls. More and more of these crackers acting like it's the Wild Wild West out here in these streets. This is genocide! They've been picking our sons and daughters off one by one—and for what? Trying to get help after a car accident? For playing with a toy in the park? For carrying a bottle of lemonade and candy?

MASON: Iced tea and *Skittles.*

KYLE: What?

MASON: It wasn't lemonade. It was iced tea.

KYLE: Nigga, I don't care if it was a goddamn forty-ounce and a blunt! They are killing them for being black!

MASON: The details matter. The truth does matter. The facts matter. We can't lose our principles just because—

KYLE: Just because? Don't tell me what matters! Black lives matter, motherfucker! What matters is that a black man dies at the hands of the enemy every thirty-six hours. These fools are using our bodies for target practice and our souls for worse. Those are my principles!

MASON: Is it always so simple? So black and white? You've never had one moment of doubt? A second of wavering? You never wondered just once if your way is the right way?

KYLE: No, I haven't. Never.

MASON: You're going to tell me that you're absolutely sure what you'd do in any instance?

KYLE: I've got to be sure.

MASON: So, if you got a call that someone had a gun in a park where kids are playing you wouldn't act right away? Remember you've got one in the chamber. You're hyped up and ready to defend everybody who you think is in danger.

KYLE: A danger to who? It was a toy gun!

MASON: With the safety tip torn off! In that split second a scared man had to decide whether to be a hero for all those innocent people on that playground or take the risk of being a villain for taking the life of the wrong person.

KYLE: Not just a wrong person. A child. A little boy. You and I both know he should have, no he would have taken just a few seconds to make sure of the situation if that child was blue-eyed with blonde hair. Are there any dead white children with toy guns you know about? Let me know.

MASON: Louisiana. A couple of years ago. Cops lit up a car with an unarmed white man and his six-year-old son. The son died. He was autistic.

KYLE: OK. Yeah. I heard about that case. It's not comparable. Those cops—

MASON: Two black cops.

KYLE: Yeah those two black cops didn't know he was even in the car! He's no poster child for reverse police brutality! I bet you can't name a black cop who has murdered a white child while looking him in the face. By the way, those cops have been charged with attempted murder.

MASON: I know that!

KYLE: Well, do you know that black men are twenty-one times more likely to be killed by police than white ones?

MASON: Of course I do! That's criminal, but I can't let that define my life.

KYLE: Ain't nobody talking about individual lives. I'm talking about the collective.

MASON: I just think some of those stats are a little exaggerated.

KYLE: You got me messed up! Come the hell on, Dix! We are being slaughtered! Not just by the fuckin' police but by random crazies who feel completely empowered to do so! We can't let this stand. From Emmett Till to Trayvon Martin. It's got to stop.

MASON: There will always be ugliness, scared white people, and racism. That's not new. We need to continue to vote for progressive leadership, march to protest injustices, and push the federal and local courts to be accountable for—

KYLE [*simultaneously*]: Aw, man. You done changed up. I don't even believe you're talking this mess. You done gone way past selling out, kid. The voting booth? The courts? Marching? [*Laughing*] What century are you living in? That shit's done, brotha. They stay stealing elections and they're turning the clock back every day in the courts. Those old methods are for history books and that new museum they let the Negroes have to house their dead and their memories of greatness. I don't need it. My heroes are all living.

MASON: I guess these new tactics will set us free?

KYLE: New Movement ain't playin'. If these folks want to keep talking about the nation's greatness and stand your ground they're going to find out just how shaky that ground is in this supposedly great nation.

MASON: If that's how you see it. You have your strategy. I'll stick to mine.

KYLE: One can always change course. It's never too late to self-correct. No need to stay stuck in the past. No shame in changing up your game, player.

MASON: At this point in life I'm not interested in games.

KYLE: You may not be interested but sometimes we have no choice but to play.

ACT 2

[KYLE *and* MASON *are sitting at the dining-room table, listening to the voice of a female newscaster.*]

VOICE-OVER: To recap, this Nor'easter will rage for another twelve to twenty-four hours with snowfall totals for New York's Capital District exceeding two feet. Albany International Airport is closing due to poor visibility and ice. Amtrak service is limited and they expect service disruption during the height of the storm. Authorities advise everyone to avoid unnecessary—

[MASON *turns off the computer.*]

KYLE: Shit! It sounds like a war zone out there! I don't know how you fuck with this. I should have brought my boots.

MASON: Yeah. Well this isn't exactly gator weather.

KYLE [*both start laughing*]: Fuck you, Dix! I like my gators.

MASON: You need to get your ass back home to that Cali sunshine.

KYLE: How do you deal with this cold? This is some straight up Nordic shit!

MASON: I'm used to it. [*Holding his empty glass up to the light*] Sorry, I'm a terrible host. Another drink?

KYLE: Sounds like one's in order. Hit me.

MASON [*making drinks*]: Don't let the weather get to you. It should be cool by morning. Fresh snow is kinda nice. So pure, soft, and full of light.

KYLE: It looks cold, white, and sterile to me. I just hope I can get out of here in the morning. I'd hate to be trapped in this place.

MASON: We'll have to see

[MASON *hands* KYLE *a drink.*]

KYLE: I'm digging this exposed brick.

MASON: Thanks.

KYLE: You don't see that too often in Cali.

MASON: Renovating an old brownstone will kick your ass. Hunting around for original pieces and picking out paint colors. Despite all that, the act of reclaiming this place calms me.

KYLE: Nice hobby if you got the time and money. How old is this place?

MASON: Old as dirt.

KYLE: Didn't I see a plaque outside?

MASON: From the Historic Albany Foundation. It certifies that the brownstone was built in eighteen fifty-five.

KYLE: Eighteen fifty fuckin' five? Damn! Could a brotha even own a house back then? I know he could have been owned—

MASON [*begining to show his pride*]: That's right. Well, you're going to love this. This house was once a stop on the Underground Railroad.

KYLE: What?

MASON [*pointing to a framed newspaper article about the house's historical significance*]: My home was a way station. It's amazing to think that folks use to hide here. It's kind of strange when I see people outside my window on that Underground Railroad tour. They take pictures. Sometimes they cry.

KYLE: Nothing like a little guilt to bring on the tears of white liberals. So, all you gotta do is drop a little cash and you too can own a piece of black history?

MASON: That's rather simplistic.

KYLE: You gonna get all sensitive on me? Come on, don't you feel some kinda way about that shit?

MASON: Why shouldn't I own it?

KYLE: It's your money, bro. Do what you want with it.

MASON: It was a stop on the Underground Railroad! Would you rather see it in the hands of somebody else? How would you feel if someone owned it who knows nothing about our history or the significance of this house? What if they just tore it down? Is that better? Should we bury our shameful past?

KYLE: It ain't our shame. I don't care who owns it, I'm just saying that it's a damn shame that our history is so cheap. Do the black people who live here even care about that historic designation? What does it get them? You know what? Fuck history. I'm here to change the future for the living.

MASON: History is all that we know for sure. The future is just a promise and a hope. I fell in love with this house because of its history. It was drafty and neglected. Got it dirt cheap. If I didn't snatch it up somebody else would have. I love this place. I upgraded the electrical and plumbing, put in new windows, refinished the floors, and installed a professional-grade kitchen. Now it's our palace—a respite from the city.

KYLE: This is sacred space, Dix.

MASON: Don't you think I know that?

KYLE: Almost like a graveyard.

MASON: If it is a graveyard, it's one that I loved back into life. Now it's a garden. It's a living testament to our survival. It's history. Do you realize that slaves—

KYLE: Enslaved Africans.

MASON: Runaway slaves—

KYLE: You mean, self-liberated peoples of African descent?

MASON: Whatever you want to call them. Our ancestors found refuge here, in this house. My house. When you own the past it can't hurt you, it can't control you, and it certainly can't bury you.

KYLE: So, all it takes is the pride of ownership?

MASON: It counts for something, especially for people whose ancestors were once owned. Sometimes I think about who lived in this house before me and what they did. They weren't armchair revolutionaries. They put it all on the line.

KYLE: OK. Let me see it! Show me the secret hideaway spot. Where is this stop on the Underground Railroad?

MASON: Nothing to see really—just a small crawl space in the attic.

KYLE: Big enough to hide a grown man?

MASON: A malnourished man or a woman and a small child.

KYLE: Damn.

MASON: Yeah.

KYLE: So, would you do it if you had the chance?

MASON: Do what? Hide a runaway? Help somebody steal away to freedom?

KYLE: You say that like it's a joke. Would you risk your life, your freedom, to free others?

MASON: That's not a question I need to answer. Slavery is over now.

KYLE: Is it? You sure about that? The way they got folks working day in and day out you can hardly tell.

MASON: That's capitalism.

KYLE: That's exploitation, brother. You seem far from those days when you were quoting Malcolm and reading *Revolutionary Suicide*!

MASON: I've moved beyond rhetoric. I'm a man of action.

KYLE: What are your actions these days?

MASON: Oh, I got to provide receipts in my own house?

KYLE: Yeah. Let's see 'em.

MASON: Listen, man, I put in my work where my heart is. I tutor fifth graders on reading and math. I coach basketball at the Boys & Girls Club during the fall, softball in the spring, and in the summer I sponsor a swim team so maybe there won't be so many black kids drowning every year. I also volunteer with the Bard College Prison Initiative.

KYLE: Wow. Impressive. Are you running for Saint Bourgie?

MASON: I'm not running for shit. I don't need a title or fans. I know I'm changing the world.

KYLE: Fair enough. I appreciate what you're doing—really. Especially for those brothas who are locked up. But you've got more to give. With your gifts you can contribute on an even larger scale.

MASON: I don't need a larger scale, K. Those kids know me. They say, "Hey, Mr. Dixon, what's it like to be a lawyer? I want to be one someday." That's saving lives, K. That's revolutionary. When I show up at that prison to teach those brothers they are sitting in class hungry to be fed. These men show up ready to tear apart everything I bring them. It wouldn't take them six or seven years to finish college if they were born into privilege. You may be thinking about slavery, but you see I've got my mind on the new Jim Crow.

KYLE: Sounds pretty safe to me. I guess you just let somebody else take the true weight while you get all the applause, huh?

MASON: Well, I think I've taken all the weight I need to carry in this lifetime.

[MASON *begins cleaning up his work-area books and files. A text comes in.* MASON *reads it, then furiously responds.*]

KYLE [*looking out the window at the snow*]: You got a piece?

MASON: What?

KYLE: You packing? You got a gun? A firearm. Shit. Staying up here in all this whiteness I'd need me an arsenal.

MASON: Harriet doesn't like guns.

KYLE: Does she know her namesake carried heat? Black Moses never would have freed so many if she wasn't packing some serious—

MASON: She's well aware of the history of her namesake. Why? You came up here strapped—

KYLE: Man, chill. I'm just making conversation.

[KYLE *looks at a photograph on the mantel. It is a picture of* MASON *with a beautiful fair skinned African American woman who could pass for white. She appears ten years younger than* MASON.]

Besides I wouldn't want to upset pretty Miss Harriet. This is your woman?

MASON: Yeah.

KYLE: Well damn! Good for you. [*Studying another picture of Harriet alone*] She's fine! A sista?

MASON: What? Yes, a sista.

KYLE: You checked her DNA? She looks kinda—

MASON: One hundred percent black woman.

KYLE: OK. I stand corrected. I thought when you made partner they gave you a white girl as a gift. "Here's Becky!"

MASON: Man, kiss my black ass!

KYLE: Chill. So where is this one hundred percent black woman on this dreary, cold, snowy ass night?

MASON: Harriet stayed in the city tonight. She has enough sense to stay out of raging storms.

KYLE: Good for her. So, what does Miss Harriet do? She an uptight lawyer too?

MASON: *Dr.* Harriet teaches black history at Columbia.

KYLE: Oh, she definitely knows her Tubman then. You always liked smart chicks!

MASON: Smart women are sexy.

KYLE: If she's at Columbia, she must be sexy as hell. That's a long-ass commute though.

MASON: We stay in the city during the week. We have a little place in Harlem.

KYLE: Of course you do. I'd stay there too if I was her. Dr. Harriet picks that high cotton. Is she satisfied she hooked with up a member of the 100 Black Men who hands out scholarships and Thanksgiving turkeys to lowly Cullad folk?

MASON: K, it doesn't matter how you try to come at me. I'm supposed to be ashamed of what I've earned? What I've become? You never seem too pressed about what your folks gave you. My family is proud of everything I've accomplished. After what my uncle went through? No, they don't see any upside to prison. They want me to be a free black man.

KYLE: So, are you free? You a free man?

MASON: Yes, I'm free.

KYLE: You a free man of color and a Negro of means.

MASON: Fuck you, K!

KYLE: Don't be pissed at me. You know damn well your moms wants you to be the kind of man who knows his worth, not a man who can be bought and sold.

MASON: And what are you? Are you free?

KYLE: No, I'm not, but I'm on my way to becoming a free man. I believe we will never have true freedom until we have real power.

MASON: So, let's hear your plan. How do we get free, K?

KYLE [*holding up his glass*]: Hit me.

[MASON *pours* KYLE *and himself another shot of scotch.*]

Reparations.

MASON: Are you serious? You're starting to sound like New Movement.

KYLE: So what!

MASON: Man, that mess will get you fired before your TV contract ever gets signed.

KYLE: Wait. You can't tell me that you don't see the logic and the reasonableness of the case for reparations. Even Ta-Nehisi Coates—

MASON: Now the revolutionary is quoting *The Atlantic* to me? Wow. You must be out of Huey Newton lines!

KYLE: Say what you want but I know you read it. All you professional Negroes read and have the nerve to critique Coates so you can feel like a radical. Well I like the brotha. Besides he provided the sanitized version so our argument is palatable for middle-class consumption.

MASON: Is that right?

KYLE: They owe us. Shit! They know they owe us. That's why they're scared. It's time for them to pay up.

MASON: Let me know how that works out. I'll be here shoveling snow while you're out there shoveling—

KYLE: Shhhh! [*Places his finger to his lips. Beat.*] I know you got a good thing here and you feel proud of your contributions. I'm offering you another way to support our people without getting your hands bloody or dirty.

MASON: What you got in store for me this time, Kyle?

KYLE: It's just a small request.

MASON: Now, that would be a first.

KYLE: It's right up your alley. Help me craft a document . . . a contract so to speak—for reparations that can be used to negotiate our terms. Think of it as crafting a bill for what we are owed.

MASON: Why do you need me, Mr. Revolutionary? Sounds like you have everything figured out.

KYLE: I'm nothing without my treasured and talented team.

MASON: How can I forget?

KYLE: It wasn't just your finesse with words that kept you on my mind. The truth is you're the spook who sat by the door.

MASON: Wait a minute.

KYLE: Don't be insulted. Come on! You know them. You work with them day in and day out. You know how they think. You know how they move. You know how they put together deals—airtight. Deals that put them on top every time. You know how the house always wins? We need to be the house this time.

MASON: Not by water but the fire this time?

KYLE: We need someone who guarantees that we will win—this time for good.

MASON: A contract?

KYLE: More like a list of demands.

MASON: To insure reparations for black America?

KYLE: Money. Land. Resources.

MASON: You're crazy. You're seriously asking for reparations in this political climate?

KYLE: Ain't nobody asking for a damn thing! The days of asking are over. Nobody is going to respect you if you come to them on your knees! No. Those days are over. We are demanding—

MASON: What will you do if your *demand* for reparations fails?

KYLE: It won't. Listen, Mason, we can't remain on the defense any longer. It's time to play offense. Black folks are catching hell while a few of us enjoy fine art and Prada.

MASON: So you'll risk everything? Even prison?

KYLE: "You can jail a revolutionary, but you can't jail the revolution."

MASON: Even death?

KYLE: "My fear is not death itself, but a death without meaning." [*Taking a sip of his drink*] So 'til death do us part. I guess I'm wedded to the movement.

MASON: My uncle, the one who was in San Quentin, a few years ago he got his in the back of the head on the side of the road while on his knees with his hands in the air.

KYLE: I never knew—I'm not trying to beef with you, Dix. All I need is a simple document. What happened to you, man? You use to be a soldier.

MASON: You know what happened? I grew the fuck up! I don't need to follow you around to get women anymore. You want to know the truth? I ain't begging nobody for a got-damn thing. I'm tired. I'm sick and tired of seeing us protesting! In the streets, on TV, on social media. Shutting down freeways? Rallies? Marching! Come on, this isn't nineteen sixty-eight. Hell, it's not even nineteen eighty-eight! Mothafucka, it's twenty eighteen!

KYLE: You're damn right. This ain't nothing like sixty-eight or eighty-eight. Back in the day black folks cared about somebody other than themselves. You ain't a man. No, you're a slave trying to buy your freedom. You think you can buy yourself out of slavery? If you can, well good for you, but how can you enjoy that so-called freedom if your brothers and sisters, your woman, your mama, cousins, and friends are still in bondage? You can't buy everybody out of oppression. That's never worked. Somebody always gotta stay behind. Even the Underground Railroad couldn't take everybody for a ride. Let's talk about what they did to King! Medgar Evers! Malcolm X! Fred Hampton! George Jackson! Huey Newton! Geronimo Pratt! MOVE!

MASON: We both know Huey died over some drug shit and those folks in MOVE might as well have been a cult.

KYLE: So you gonna bury them all? Call them all crazy?

MASON: No, I'm not gonna bury them all because they aren't all dead! Elaine Brown, Assata, and Angela Davis are alive and well.

KYLE: I'm proud that those sistas are still standing [*under his breath*] of course they let the women live. But I'm talking about now. Are you paying attention to what they're doing to the young leaders? To the Dream Defenders? Black Lives Matter? And what about all those that rose up in Ferguson, in Baltimore, Oakland, New York?

MASON: I was at the protests. I'm still in the streets.

KYLE: As you should be! If you are out in these streets, then you would know that the people are leading this uprising. They're fed up. Even Amnesty International is looking at this shit! Police rolling in like militia? SWAT teams running through the hood?

MASON: It ain't the first time. There will be investigations and detailed reports that will show—

KYLE: Reports? Investigations? Man, we talking about armored tanks with police tear-gassing protesters standing in their own front yards! These kids are soldiers! They keep coming by the busloads. Hoodies up and straight to jail—after a few kicks to the head. Maybe even a bullet in the back. They ain't worried. This generation has real heart. They are soldiers that refuse to back down.

MASON: I guess you support that new group?

KYLE: New Movement? I do. They're the true soldiers in this war, my brotha!

MASON: War? Man, you know you're talking about bloodshed, right? Armed insurrection?

KYLE: If need be.

MASON: You really want a race war?

KYLE: Me? Come on, you know we've been losing a race war for the past four hundred years. I'm talking about fighting back and winning this time. Listen, Dix, we need folks with your skills to help us craft a document, a policy that will lay out the parameters—

MASON: I'm an officer of the court. You know what kind of precarious situation you're putting me in? I thought you were getting deeper into this shit. You're crazy!

KYLE: Crazy? Crazy is expecting black people to get up every morning, go to work and move peacefully through a world that despises them. Every day black folks go the grocery store, the gym, the dry cleaner, and some demoralizing job like all is well. No wonder so many of us end up at the liquor store every night or hitting up the dope man. If you ask me, crazy is what proves that you're sane.

MASON: It doesn't matter how you justify this. This movement is dangerous and crazy—

KYLE: Know what? It doesn't matter what you call me. And I don't give a fuck how nice your house is, how big your whip is, or how light-skinned your bitch is—

MASON: Nigga, watch your mouth!

KYLE: Hey! All I know is you ain't nothing but a boy until you're ready to die, like a black man. I hustle, same as you, but I hustle for us.

MASON: It's easy for you to say that. You weren't born on welfare, forced to scratch for everything you got.

KYLE: Ain't nobody out here romanticizing poverty.

MASON: You're always after somebody else to put their life on the line. You living pretty damn well yourself!

KYLE: You best believe my life is sweet, but I'm trying to get us to a place where everyone can live well. How can you sleep at night when there is a brother who looks like you but he's broke and on the street?

MASON: Some of us have better because some of us do better. If he was like me? Really like me, his ass would not be broke! And you know what? I could care less if they see me as a man, or a fuckin' baboon! It only matters to me what I see when I look in the mirror. When I put on my suit and tie each morning. I love who I see. I'm a proud black man. I hustle for me and you know what? I grind everyday. Everybody wins.

KYLE: You can't mean that. Stop drinking that scotch cause it's messing up your head. You got this twisted. Listen, I understood back in the day when we shut down campus—

MASON [*speaking over* KYLE]: I'm not trying to stroll down memory lane with you.

KYLE [*talking over* MASON]: to force the dean to divest was merely a training ground to teach us how to shut down something greater. It's time to execute the next phase of the plan.

MASON: Well the way I see it we need to be more strategic and institute some twenty-first century tactics. I mean use the mighty dollar to make those in power bend to our will. Nothing else matters in this country. It never has, it never will.

KYLE: Wow. Everything I taught you comes out of your mouth dead wrong.

MASON: Taught me? That you taught me? Well, how about this? What's in the briefcase, K?

KYLE: Nothing you need to worry about, Mr. Dixon. Nothing at all.

ACT 3

[*Flashback to 1988. The BSA office. Night.* KYLE *is putting away a chessboard.*]

KYLE: Checkmate! You surprised me, young blood.

MASON: Can't believe I almost beat you, huh?

KYLE: No, I can't believe you got a bunch of Kappas to attend an anti-apartheid rally!

MASON: I can do even more.

KYLE: Is that right? What you ready for, young blood?

MASON: Anything.

KYLE: Anything? OK. I've got a small, quick, but important task.

MASON: Whatever you need. Just tell me what it is.

KYLE: I'm not sure. This is a delicate situation. We need someone absolutely trustworthy. It's important that we select a dude who isn't on academic probation and has never been in trouble with the law.

MASON: I'm good on both fronts.

KYLE: Cool, because this is dangerous. I know that your cash is lean but I'm sure I can get my pops to contribute the dough to help you make bail if it comes to that.

MASON: The judge? Wow. That's great because my moms doesn't have the cash to—

KYLE: Don't you worry, little brother. Just remember that Huey P. Newton said, "There can be no prison which can hold our movement down."

MASON: Right. And you're sure your father will do that—pay the bail if something goes wrong?

KYLE: Trust me. I'll make sure.

MASON: Then I'm fine. It's not that I'm afraid of prison, but it would kill my mom if I ended up—

KYLE: Stop worrying. Nothing will go wrong.

MASON: I appreciate your help. Your parents are golden—

KYLE: They love you like you're one of their own. They see you as the obedient son they wish they had! Besides, I'm sure you'd do me a solid if you could. Who knows what the future holds? You may have to bail my ass out one day!

MASON: You know I would.

[*Handshake.*]

KYLE: I believe that.

MASON: You can always count on me.

KYLE: Well I found a new way to capture the president's attention.

[*Pause.* KYLE *spreads a campus map on the desk.*]

You know Founders' Hall?

MASON: Of course. What about it?

KYLE: I think it's best that we hit 'em where they live, so to speak. [*Pointing to map*] You know this statue in front?

MASON: Yeah.

KYLE: Come by for dinner with me and my folks. They will be our alibi. After they go to the den to watch the news, you sneak out and head to campus. There will be a key there tonight after ten P.M. Grab it and unlock the back door to the registrar's office. The alarm will be off.

MASON: You sure?

KYLE: Yes, I'm sure. You're going to deliver a package. The instructions will be with the key.

MASON: Got it. Key at the statue. Registrar's office. Drop the package.

KYLE: Then dash like you're Carl Lewis and meet me back at my parents' house. I'll let you in the back, they won't know you ever left.

MASON: Got it.

KYLE: You understand the immense importance of this task?

MASON: Yes. [*Pause*] Nobody will get hurt, right?

KYLE [*grabbing him gently by the shoulders*]: We're not animals, Dix. We are not the ones treating people like subhumans and second-class citizens in their own homeland. We just want to push some of the president's buttons a little.

MASON [*nervously*]: OK.

KYLE: Don't worry.

MASON: I'm not worried. No, I can do this.

[KYLE *retrieves the package and hands it to* MASON.]

What's in it?

KYLE: Don't worry about that either. No need for you to know. It's best for everybody concerned if we keep um . . . certain elements in the dark.

MASON: If you say so.

KYLE: Cool. [*Beat*] Dix, I'm counting on you to come through.
MASON: I told you. I can handle whatever you need.
KYLE: This stays between us. Only us. Nobody else can ever know. Never.
MASON: Understood.
KYLE: Never. Be careful. [*They shake hands.*]

[*Present.* MASON *comes downstairs from his room, reading from his cell phone.* KYLE *is checking something in his briefcase when he notices* MASON *has returned and suddenly snaps it shut.*]

MASON: Twitter is lit up. Looks like the authorities have some leads on the New Movement leader.
KYLE: Is that right?
MASON: It won't be long now.
KYLE: They'll catch him.
MASON: Or her?
KYLE: And another leader will take "her" place. No assassinations or prison can stop this.
MASON: I can't believe you admire those nuts. I thought you'd feel in competition with them. They're getting all the shine these days.
KYLE: Naw. We all want the same thing. I have no problem with New Movement. If he's caught—
MASON: Or she?
KYLE: If a leader is caught they will be a legend. But the truth is they are a leaderless group—this generation learned from the failures of the past. Leader or no leader, the revolution has captured the attention of a nation.
MASON: Seems like they came out of nowhere.
KYLE: No brotha, a movement this strong doesn't spring up overnight. Folks have been training—
MASON: Training?
KYLE: Yeah, training! Don't you realize that a significant number of black folks make up the armed forces in the U-S of A? They've been teaching our folks what they know about weaponry, hand-to-hand combat, even explosives. They've been off the grid reading. Writing. Waiting.
MASON: They're straight bombing shit. How are they gonna combat the US? They'll be slaughtered.

KYLE: If you can't beat the enemy gun for gun, then you have to use other means like guerrilla warfare and—

MASON: You know everyone thinks they're terrorists?

KYLE: Don't forget they called Mandela a terrorist too but now he's seen as a hero—

MASON: Oh, so these cats are the ANC? And their leader is Mandela two-point-oh?

KYLE: This is about agency! It's about making folks recognize that there can never be peace without payment. How can something so fucked up not deserve even an apology? How can we expect to go on without receiving what is due us? Even King said that America's check was marked insufficient funds!

MASON: Don't you realize we will never be made whole—no matter how much they give us? Being whole again, that's up to us.

KYLE: I don't need them to make us whole. I sure as hell don't trust them with our souls, but that doesn't mean they shouldn't pay! We can't allow them to wipe the slate clean!

MASON: So, you want bloodshed?

KYLE: I want blood money.

MASON: Money. The very evil you accuse me of pursuing?

KYLE: We didn't create the evil, Dix. But yes, money. That's what they understand and after being in this wilderness of America it seems it's all we understand too. The money will allow us to negotiate on a more equal footing. Money and land. Reparations.

MASON: So how much? How much money for your lynched great uncle? How many acres for your raped great-great-grandmother? Your tortured and sold great granddaddy? How much for the last dude murdered in the street by a scared cop?

KYLE: More than forty acres and a mule! Something much more than—

MASON: Affirmative action and welfare checks?

KYLE: Didn't affirmative action get your ass into law school? It wasn't a problem then.

MASON: I didn't get in through affirmative action!

KYLE: That's what those white boys think when they see your black ass walking around that firm. I know you hate that shit. You know you have no real power or control even as a partner. Power is all they know and all they respect. That's the only thing that gets America's attention.

MASON: You admitting that black folks are Americans?

KYLE: We will never be true Americans but here we are trapped in this nightmare with the ones who dragged us here. We built this country and now we gonna get what we deserve. This country is ours. We must demand and if necessary take what is due to us. Ain't nobody on their knees anymore. We ain't begging for nothing. We are demanding what's ours.

MASON: Is this why you're here? To recruit me? Is this what our reunion is really about?

KYLE: Good soldiers with experience are hard to find. The Panthers are either buried in exile or still doing time. That leaves men like you who have been on the sidelines too long.

MASON: So tell me the truth. You're with New Movement, huh?

KYLE: Like I said, I admire what they stand for. Power, respect, and truth.

MASON: You're involved with those crazy motherfuckers?

KYLE: I won't denounce them.

MASON: And their tactics?

KYLE: Bold. Precise. Unforgettable.

MASON: Bomb first, negotiate later? And their demands?

KYLE: Just what they owe us.

MASON: Reparations are just another form of welfare.

KYLE: What?

MASON: The fight for reparations just keeps us focused on them. They aren't the only source of power. Why are you looking for handouts from those who see you as subhuman? That's crazy!

KYLE: There goes that word again. It lacks nuance. You should find something else to describe the audacious black man who fights for his freedom.

MASON: Do you know them? The leaders?

KYLE: Let's just say over the years I've urged New Movement to consider the next phase in the struggle for black liberation. It's been wonderful to see them carry out my—

MASON: Orders?

KYLE: My philosophy. My suggestions have been embraced and—

MASON: No wonder you're not jealous. You're the one. Is the FBI after you? Damn.

[*It hits him like a load of bricks.*]

So, you're in charge? You're New Movement. [*Beat*] Don't you know you're gonna kill somebody if this keeps up? You know history. Innocent black people will burn because of you.

KYLE: You worried? Afraid they're going to start targeting uppity, sell-out Negroes?

MASON: Like your family?

KYLE: It's not about what I was born into. It's what I became. I'm a man of my people more than you've ever been. You've always wanted to distance yourself from the black folks you came up with. Isn't that why you were always hanging out at my crib with my folks?

MASON: I won't apologize for accepting love and support from your parents. You're wrong. I never wanted to distance myself from black folks, just poverty. What would you know about that? You've never been hungry. Never had to stay in a shelter and stay up all night making sure nobody rolled up on you and your mother in the dark. So yes, I wanted to be as far away from poor as possible. Why wouldn't I? Know this, whatever happens I'll survive. But I don't want any part of what you're planning. Not this time.

KYLE: Have you changed that much, Dix? Were you just fronting back in the day? Wasn't it you who was so eager to bomb the registrar's office as a form of symbolic justice!

MASON: Hold up, slick! I just delivered a package for my homie! Back then I was just another one of your dedicated followers.

KYLE: Didn't one of your speeches talk about bringing down the empire brick by brick, Dix?

MASON: There is no more Dix! This is Mason's law. Dix is gone. He's my past. I always wondered about old ass men with nicknames. Poppy, Daddy, Chuy, Biggie, Diddy. What's your name, man? Fuck what your boys call you. What's the name your mama gave you? That woman who first bled for you? That's your name. I'm Mason and you are Kyle. No more. No less.

KYLE: You've been calling me K for thirty years. Still calling me K. Nicknames ain't childish. They're about history. Friendship. Connection. Blackness. Black people are suffering right outside your beautifully restored nineteenth-century door.

MASON: Blackness? Is this about blackness? You want to know the truth? Sometimes I hate blackness. Sometimes I even hate black people. All the problems and burdens and traumatic shit. I'm tired, man. Do you get that? I just want to be free of all that history and struggle.
KYLE: That's why we are asking for an end to it. Now.
MASON: There is no dignity in pleading.
KYLE: But there is dignity is fighting.
MASON: You don't get to choose for the rest of us.
KYLE: But that's what a real leader does.

[KYLE *walks over to the chess set and inspects the pieces.*]

Beautiful set.
MASON: Thanks.
KYLE: Marble?

[MASON *nods.*]

You always did like nice shit. This set up here just for show? Or do you still play?
MASON: Unfortunately, I don't have time for games anymore. It's more for show.
KYLE: So, let's play. If I win then you join New Movement and give us what we need for as long as we need you. If you win I leave you in peace to your beautiful MLK inspired dream.
MASON: That's a hell of a wager.
KYLE [*dusting off the black king*]: Yeah. And let's play hustler style like we did when we were kids.
MASON: Sure. Fuck it! Let's go.
KYLE: Show me what you've got left, old man. You still got game?
MASON: I'll let you be the judge of that. You're the guest so you choose. [*Removing a timer from a kitchen drawer*] So do you want to be white?
KYLE: No, man. That's all you. You know I've always got to be black.
MASON: Of course. I'm not afraid to be white. Black it is.

[MASON *sets up the chessboard.* MASON *and* KYLE *play speed chess quietly but intensely, using the timer.*]

KYLE: You're better than I remember.
MASON: I play chess every day. I'm an attorney.

KYLE: Do you wonder what your partners would think if they knew what you did back in the day?

MASON: Everybody knows I was a student activist. I was part of a morally sound crusade.

KYLE: The crusade was very moral, but your actions? Not much different from New Movement if you ask me.

MASON: You aren't about to blackmail me into anything—besides, nobody will believe you.

KYLE: Maybe not, but I think they will believe their eyes.

MASON: What are talking about, man?

KYLE: I'm talking about a video. The surveillance footage from the registrar's office.

MASON: So? What's that got to do with me?

KYLE: My dad had friends in high places.

MASON: Again, what's that got to do with me?

KYLE: Yeah, I think you know. How do you think that all went away back in the day? My family has always been there for you, Dix. We've been keeping it safe, on your behalf of course.

MASON: If you wanted to take care of me, you would have destroyed anything that could incriminate me. I'm supposed to be your homeboy, right?

KYLE: Well, let's just say I had a lot more than looking out for you in mind. This doesn't have to be ugly. I'm just here for help. I'm asking for our people: Will you help us?

MASON: No. Give me the tape—if there really is one.

KYLE: Oh, there's a tape. You're a lawyer. You know the statute of limitations is still open for something like this. What would happen if the authorities happened to come upon such a treasure? All it takes is a few seconds to upload a video and the world will know who you really are, Dix.

MASON: Give it to me.

KYLE: Now it's my turn to say no.

MASON: Homeboys don't blackmail each other, but I guess your kind of revolution includes extortion.

KYLE: Don't blame me! You pushed me to this! You know what I'm asking is important. More important than a career. Even more important than brotherhood.

MASON: I can't believe this is happening.
KYLE: You forced me to go there.
MASON: So you'd destroy me?
KYLE: This shit is simple. You're either with or against the people. We need you. Join us.
MASON: Give me the tape.
KYLE: I'm more than happy to oblige. I just need you to pledge your loyalty. Just help us get our people off our knees once and for all.
MASON: I'm not playing with you, K.
KYLE: But I am playing and this game is real. You have skills that New Movement needs. You once had the heart to act. If not for your old friend, then do it for the love of our people. You still remember love, don't you?
MASON: Checkmate! Fuck you, K! Take your shit and leave my house. I don't care if you freeze out there or if the FBI, CIA, or NSA finds your ass. Go ahead and show the damn tape to whoever you like. I don't need to prove shit to you or anyone else at this point in my life. I'll take my chances. I'm not about to—

[*There is a loud knock at the door.*]

MASON [*Beat*]: Yes! Who is it?

[*No one answers but the knocking continues.*]

Who is it?
KYLE: It looks like they're here.

[*He picks up the briefcase slowly.*]

What are you willing to die for, Dix?

[*The knocking intensifies.*]

[*Darkness.* KYLE *and* MASON *are in shadow, facing each other as they did at the play's opening.*]

[*The knocking continues for a few more beats.*]

[*Then silence.*]

MONROE

This is a cursed valley,
ask the broken mules, the swollen children,
ask the dried women, their gap-toothed men,
ask the parish priest, who, in the altarpiece,
carries a replica of the church,
ask the two who could be Eve and Adam dancing.

—Derek Walcott, "For the Altarpiece of the Roseau Valley Church, Saint Lucia"

Monroe is dedicated to the memory of George Bolden, an illiterate black man accused of writing a lewd note to a white woman, who was lynched near Monroe, Louisiana, on April 30, 1919.

DEVELOPMENT HISTORY

Cherríe Moraga directed a staged reading of *Monroe* on June 2, 1997, at BRAVA! Theatre for Women in the Arts in San Francisco with the following cast: Tanya Mayo as Cherry Henry, Yvonne Price as Ma Henry, Sterling K. Brown as Clyde James, Ryan Michelle Bathé as Viola Henry, Berwick Haynes as Dr. Wyland and Seymour Jones, and Ricardo Bracho as the narrator.

Monroe won the 2018 Austin Playhouse Festival of New Texas Plays. On April 29, 2018, Lara Toner Haddock directed a staged reading with Taji Senior as Cherry Henry, Carla Nickerson as Ma Henry, Huck Huckaby as Dr. Wyland, Delante Keys as Clyde James, Marc Pouhé as Seymour Jones, and Crystal Bird Caviel as Viola Henry.

PRODUCTION HISTORY

Monroe had its world premiere at the Austin Playhouse (Don Toner, Producing Artistic Director; Lara Toner Haddock, Artistic Director) on September 7, 2018, in Austin, Texas. The production manager was Barry Miller, with set design by Mike Toner, costume design by Diana Huckaby, lighting design by Chris Conard, and sound design by Robert Fisher. The properties designer was Jennifer Singletary. Lara Toner Haddock directed the following cast:

Cherry Henry . . . . Deja Morgan
Ma Henry . . . . Carla Nickerson
Dr. Wyland. . . . . Huck Huckaby
Clyde James . . . . Kriston Woodreaux
Seymour Jones . . . . Marc Pouhé
Viola Henry . . Crystal Bird Caviel, Taji Senior, Lisa B. Thompson

CHARACTERS

Cherry Henry, black girl, twenty-one, domestic/cook.
Ma Henry, black woman, late seventies, family matriarch, Cherry's grandmother.
Dr. Wyland, white man, late-fifties, general physician.
Clyde James, black man, twenty-nine, factory worker.
Seymour Jones, black man, mid-forties, bartender.
Viola Henry, black woman, twenty-seven, blues singer, Cherry's cousin.

SETTING

September 1946. Monroe, Louisiana, in Ouachita (pronounced WAH-shi-tah) Parish, the location of the fifth-highest number of lynchings in the United States from 1877 to 1950. Ma Henry's neighborhood has no sidewalks. All of the one-story homes have porches and are built on bricks so that they do not flood when the Ouachita River rises. Lots of fig trees abound, and even in early fall Monroe's thick, humid air smells heavy like ripe fruit.

PLAYWRIGHT'S NOTE

This a realist play with magical elements. The beliefs of each character must be honored and delivered with sincerity. The play opens with a body hanging in a tree but the audience does not actually see the body. That moment allows each character to react from the standpoint of their relationship with the murdered man. There should be swift transitions between each scene and music from the period that eases transitions. Musical selections that inspired *Monroe* can also serve as excellent pre-show music:

Billie Holiday, "Strange Fruit"
Mahalia Jackson, "Take My Hand, Precious Lord"
Swan Silvertones, "O Mary, Don't You Weep"
Sister Rosetta Tharpe, "Strange Things Happening Every Day"
The War and Treaty, "Set My Soul on Fire"
Robert Johnson, "I Believe I'll Dust My Broom"
Memphis Minnie, "Me and My Chauffeur Blues"
Louis Jordan and the Tympany Five, "Choo Choo Ch'Boogie"
Charlie Parker, "Relaxin' at Camarillo"
Hoagy Carmichael, "Skylark"
Billie Holiday, "Trav'lin Light"
Louis Jordan and the Tympany Five, "Saturday Night Fish Fry"
Dizzy Gillespie, "Night in Tunisia"
The Ink Spots, "Prisoner of Love"
Nat King Cole, "(Get Your Kicks On) Route 66"
Lionel Hampton Quintet, "Hamp's Walking Boogie"
Ella Fitzgerald and the Inkspots, "I'm Beginning to See the Light"
Nina Simone, "Take Me to the Water"

ACT 1. HOME

PROLOGUE

[*Soft lights slowly come up over the dark stage, accompanied by the sound of crickets. The cast members enter one by one from different directions and stand scattered across the stage as if they are in a field. They stare silently and somberly at something in the distance. After a few beats, they begin to hum a mournful gospel tune.* CLYDE *enters and stops under the point where the rest of the cast has been gazing. He mourns what he sees. After a few beats, he embraces a body hanging from a tree. He steels himself and then cuts it down. The load falls into his hands.* CLYDE*'s actions should all be pantomimed.* CLYDE *walks off the stage slowly, carrying the body away. Once* CLYDE *leaves, the humming ceases and the crowd disperses silently in different directions. Blackout.*]

SCENE 1. COMIN' IN

[*Lights up. Late afternoon. Enter* MA HENRY *escorted by her granddaughter,* CHERRY. *They walk slowly from the road onto* MA HENRY*'s front porch. The inside of the kitchen is visible from the stage.* MA HENRY *cools herself with a church fan printed with an advertisement from the Johnson Funeral Home. Both women are dressed in black.*]

CHERRY: Why don't you sit a spell? Everybody will be 'round soon. [*Motioning to the rocking chair*] I'll bring you a big old tall glass of strawberry lemonade. [*Taking* MA HENRY*'s hat and shawl*] Would you like that? I made it from those fresh lemons—

MA HENRY: Did Clyde bring them lemons?

CHERRY: Yes, ma'am and—

MA HENRY: Then that lemonade will be sour as this day.

CHERRY: Well I'll bring you some sweet tea instead. I'm sure that will soothe you.

MA HENRY: Thank you, baby. It sure is nice to still have you by my side.

[CHERRY *goes to the kitchen and gathers a pitcher of iced tea and glasses on a tray while* MA HENRY *sits down on her rocker and takes off her shoes.*]

You always know how to make Grandma happy. Just like your brother. Oh, my sweet Jefferson. Rest his soul. [*She shakes her head.*]

CHERRY: Ma Henry, please don't get yourself all upset.

MA HENRY [*half to herself, half to* CHERRY]: Upset? I ain't gettin' myself upset! Jefferson ain't done nothin' to nobody on this here earth. And what that get him? I've never thought I'd live longer than my son. Let alone my grand. It vex me to say it, but I'm glad your mother and father ain't alive to bear this. I got a hole deeper than a well in my soul.

CHERRY: Papa always said a Negro man has gotta walk slow and listen real hard.

MA HENRY: Little Miss, don't you believe for one minute that womenfolk have it much better. We gotta move careful in this world too. Promise me you will fix it in yo' mind to make the right decisions.

CHERRY: Yes, ma'am. I promise. [*Beat*] You know I can still hear Papa's voice. He's saying that if we pray everything will be just fine.

MA HENRY: Your daddy always was wise beyond his years. No, we ain't nevah gonna give up prayin'.

CHERRY: Without the Lord we are lost.

MA HENRY: Reverend Williams sure preached over my grandson. Like he was a prince or somethin'. What a service. Just beautiful.

CHERRY: Yes, ma'am. They did right by Jefferson.

MA HENRY: Well, folks'll be here before long bringing all kinds of mischief. Cherry, you 'bout ready?

CHERRY: Yes, ma'am. I prepared almost everything before we left for the service. [*As she heads into the kitchen*] All I gotta do now is carve the turkey and bake the rolls.

MA HENRY: Make sure you got plenty of butter on them rolls, baby. Nobody likes no dry bread. Leave some room on that table 'cause folks gonna keep bringing dishes. We blessed with kind neighbors. I know one thing, that good for nothin' Clyde betta not show his face 'round this house today!

CHERRY: Why, Ma? What he done now?

MA HENRY: I'm so tired of his foolishness. [*Yelling to the kitchen*] Do you know what that Clyde asked me? "What you gonna put on his tombstone, Ma Henry?" What's wrong with that boy? Somebody ought to drag that silly fool down a road somewhere behind a bunch of well-fed horses.

CHERRY [*entering from the kitchen*]: Ma! That ain't no Christian way to talk. Why you wanna say somethin' like that?

MA HENRY: Baby, I ain't feelin' too blessed at this minute. The Lord I believe in knows my heart and will forgive me a few unkind words on a day like this one. [*Takes a sip of iced tea.*]

CHERRY: Well even with his ways, Clyde has always been good to us. We gonna need him more now than ever with Jefferson—

MA HENRY: Need him for what? Go on, baby. I'm not studyin' that Clyde James. [*Pointing toward the road to their house, from where sounds of relatives and friends arriving outside can be heard*] Here they come now. You need me to help you finish getting that spread laid out? They look hungry. [*Begins to put her shoes back on.*]

SCENE 2. TRUTH TELLIN'

[*Two months later. The waiting room of* DR. WYLAND, *in downtown Monroe. Late afternoon on a hot summer day.* DR. WYLAND *walks out of his office into the waiting room with his medical bag.* CHERRY *is waiting for him with a brown paper sack. There is a pie in the chair next to her.*]

DR. WYLAND [*annoyed*]: Excuse me?

CHERRY: Good evening, sir.

DR. WYLAND: Good evening. The office is closed for the day. What can I do for you, girl?

CHERRY: Are you Dr. Wyland?

DR. WYLAND: Yes, I am. Sorry but I'm quite busy and on my way to—

CHERRY: I brung you this. [*Hands him the pie.*]

DR. WYLAND [*hesitantly accepting*]: Oh. Thank you.

CHERRY: It's cherry pie. That was one of my daddy's favorites. Did you know Reverend Henry of True Vine?

DR. WYLAND: Reverend Henry? No, I can't say that I do.

CHERRY: Oh. I thought everybody knew my daddy.

DR. WYLAND: Well, as I was saying, I need to be on my way, Miss—

CHERRY: I'm Cherry. Cherry Henry. I was hopin' to see you today.

DR. WYLAND: See me? About what? You're not one of my patients, so—

CHERRY: Well, Mrs. Fair. I work for her. . .

DR. WYLAND: Helen? Yes, I know Mrs. Fair. Is she all right? Does she need something?

CHERRY: No, sir. She's just fine. Just fine.

DR. WYLAND: Well then?

CHERRY: Mrs. Fair talks on and on about you all the time. She says you're a very kind person. Mrs. Fair says Dr. Wyland M.D. is an excellent doctor. Mrs. Fair says—

DR. WYLAND: That's all very nice.

CHERRY: Yes, sir.

DR. WYLAND: Do thank Mrs. Fair for the pie, and if that's all, I'm on way out now. So if you don't mind—

CHERRY: Wait! I need your help! From what Mrs. Fair say, you could . . . well, you might be willing . . .

DR. WYLAND: Yes?

CHERRY: She said . . . well, um—

DR. WYLAND: Look! I'm late for an engagement and I don't have time to tarry. Perhaps you can come back tomorrow. You can speak to my nurse then and perhaps she can answer any—

CHERRY: Mrs. Fair said I should ask you my questions. That I oughta get your help. Doctor, I don't think I can sit here waiting another day. Not that your office ain't real nice and cool inside and all. I just need to talk to you now about . . .

DR. WYLAND: Girl, what is this all about exactly?

CHERRY: Exactly? [*Taking a deep breath*] I haven't seen my . . . "it"—you know—in months, and I don't know why.

DR. WYLAND: I don't understand.

CHERRY: You see, Blessed Mary came to me in a dream, I call it a vision—

DR. WYLAND: What?

CHERRY: —she told me that I had to have a baby so that He could save us, but I don't want to have a baby. I'm not married, and so that's a sin. It must be a mistake. I never. I mean I . . . No boy has ever . . .

DR. WYLAND: Ever? Ever what?

CHERRY: No boy has ever . . . what I mean is . . .

DR. WYLAND: Are you saying that you think that you're with child?

CHERRY: Yes. No. Well, I . . . don't know. [*Exasperated, pulling a pair of panties out of the paper sack*] All I know is I don't have IT no more! Mother Henry, my grandmother, says that if a lady don't have IT, then she probably gonna have ONE.

DR. WYLAND: It? [*Glancing at panties*] Yes, I see.

CHERRY: Sir? Doctor? Can you help me?

DR. WYLAND: Since Helen—uh, Mrs. Fair, referred you I will do my best for you. And this nice pie of course.

CHERRY: Thank you so much, doctor.

DR. WYLAND: Now you need to go to my examination room and get undressed.

CHERRY: What?

DR. WYLAND: I'm going to have to examine—do you understand me?

CHERRY: Yes. No . . . But, sir, ain't that proof?

DR. WYLAND: Well, not exactly. . .

CHERRY: I don't see why not. Every month, even if I'm careful my undergarments get a little dirty—just a little. It washes out just fine if I use cold water. Ever since we buried Jefferson—

DR. WYLAND: Jefferson?

CHERRY: Yes, sir. Jefferson Henry. That's my brother—

DR. WYLAND: Oh. I see. [*Noticeably uncomfortable.*]

CHERRY: Since then my stomach feels real full, not like I've been eating. It's different—and after what Holy Mary said—

DR. WYLAND: Yes, of course, Mary's vision.

CHERRY: My vision of Mary.

DR. WYLAND: Listen girl, your ideas are downright outrageous!

CHERRY: Don't worry doctor, everybody feel that way these days.

DR. WYLAND [*under his breath*]: Somehow I'm not surprised. All of that talk about Mary and visitations and what not falls out of my area of expertise. I'm a medical doctor. If we need to see about a baby I will need to check you, understand?

CHERRY [*stands still*]: I understand.

DR. WYLAND [*motioning to the door*]: Excellent! After you. I'll be in shortly once you undress.

CHERRY [*not moving*]: Yes, sir.

DR. WYLAND [*impatiently*]: Girl, will you go in the examination room and put on the gown! I don't have all night.

CHERRY: But doctor, no man's ever seen me [*whispering*] that way.

DR. WYLAND: What do you mean?

CHERRY: Without . . .

DR. WYLAND: Without what?

CHERRY: Without no clothes on and . . . [*whispers*] seen down there. I'm a Christian girl.

DR. WYLAND: Well, if that's true, then you can't be having a child. Our business is done right now.

CHERRY: Are you sure, even after Mary?

DR. WYLAND: I've been a doctor for twenty-eight years. I have presided over the births of at least a thousand babies in Ouachita Parish—

CHERRY: A thousand?

DR. WYLAND: Yes! Big ones, small ones, fat ones, long ones. Babies that cried as soon as they were born and others that needed a little pat on the rump, but you know the one thing that they all had in common, Miss—

CHERRY: Cherry, Cherry Henry.

DR. WYLAND: Miss Cherry, is that they all had a daddy. I must tell you: no man, no baby.

CHERRY: Oh . . .

DR. WYLAND: Now that's just my expert medical opinion. But if you still want me to examine you—

CHERRY [*standing*]: Naw! No, sir . . . that's all right. Sorry to bother you. Thank you, Dr. Wyland!

DR. WYLAND: Excellent! I'll be on my way then. Thanks again for the pie.

CHERRY: You're very welcome, Doctor.

DR. WYLAND [*picking up his medical bag and escorting* CHERRY *to the door*]: Oh, and tell Mrs. Fair I'll see her at next week's bridge game. Good evening.

CHERRY: Yes, sir. I sure will tell her. Evening.

[CHERRY *exits with a bewildered look on her face.* DR. WYLAND *follows. Lights fade.*]

SCENE 3. GETTIN' SUMPIN'

[*Late morning, the next day.* CHERRY *is peeling apples for baking pies in* MA HENRY*'s kitchen. She's singing a hymn to herself softly. The kitchen screen door squeaks loudly.* CLYDE *enters, carrying a basket of pecans.*]

CLYDE [*to himself*]: Need ta get that do' fixed. [*Loudly to her*] Hey, Miss Cherry! How you doin' on this fine day?

CHERRY: I'm good. And you? [*Distracted, returns to chopping apples*]

CLYDE [*looking around*]: Good, good. Sure do smell like heaven up in here, lady.

CHERRY: Hmm.

CLYDE [*placing the basket down*]: I brung you these pecans from Miss Bernadine's place.

CHERRY: You late! I asked for them early this mornin'. Clyde, why you always late?

CLYDE: Sorry, Cherry. As far as I can see don't nothin' get here on time but trouble. [*Laughs, then pausing once he doesn't get a reply*] You goin' over to the revival tonight?

CHERRY: What you think I'm doin' all this bakin' for? Don't be askin' me no silly questions, Clyde James. You know I got a whole lot to do!

CLYDE: Just tryin' to make a little conversation, girl.

CHERRY: Hmm. Well while you here why don't you shell some of them pecans.

CLYDE [*tipping his hat*]: Yes, ma'am. [*Gets second wind of enthusiasm, picks up the nutcracker, and starts shelling*] I hear that Reverend Barker gonna be here all the way from Galveston. True Vine's gonna put on some serious church. Barker sure does know how to lay folks out. He gives you an ear full, then kicks you in the shins for good measure. [*Chuckles.*]

CHERRY [*seriously*]: Ain't nothin' like the word. God sings to us from the good book. The way these times are goin' folks need that song more than ever. Yes, ain't nothin' like the word. [*Pause*] Sometimes I just wish—

CLYDE: What?

CHERRY: I just wish it wasn't so loud. The choir, the preacher. Seems like everybody be trying to compete with God. Sometimes I like to hear myself pray in the quiet. I like to light a candle and pray.

CLYDE: That sounds like some ole' Hoodoo mess. Your daddy didn't raise you that way.

CHERRY [*stops working*]: Ain't nothin' particular 'bout it. I'm not talkin' about a bunch of African stuff, I mean saintly quiet. Prayer. [*Starts sifting flour*] You don't understand nothin' no way so forget it.

CLYDE: You need to watch out for them white folks. They got you talkin' real peculiar like.

CHERRY: Mind your business about what I'm doin', mister! Besides, you got plenty of business of ya own don't you?

CLYDE: Yes, ma'am.

[CLYDE *continues to shell pecans while* CHERRY *rolls dough; they work in a heavy silence while* CLYDE *regularly glances at her.*]

CHERRY: So, how's work at Peterson's?

CLYDE: Shoot! I ain't lettin' them people get under my skin. They tell ya to pick that up, run here, tote that there, set that down then do it all over again. I do what I need to and leave the rest alone. Old man Peterson and his boys are crazy out they minds. Do you know that if you late one minute they won't pay you but half a day?

CHERRY: No matter what time you get there? Naw, that ain't right.

CLYDE: Last week Billy was tryin' to talk to the old man about his pay and the next day he showed up lookin' mighty wrinkled, know what I mean?

CHERRY: What you saying?

CLYDE: Talkin' 'bout how wicked they are. His face was swollen, lip busted, and his eye was blacker than a nightmare.

CHERRY: Can't worry 'bout it long as you gettin' your wages. It's the only place to work 'round here anyway. Just stay out of it and pray.

CLYDE: Tell that to somebody who plan to be 'round this town forever.

CHERRY: What you talkin' 'bout? You gonna leave Monroe?

CLYDE: Yes, ma'am. Got to get out of this place. Not quite yet. I'm waiting a bit 'cause I need to rest up and save me some money. Got me a real long journey ahead.

[CLYDE *discovers a bottle of cooking sherry on the pantry shelf and starts to read the label.*]

CHERRY: What you want with that?

CLYDE: Did I say I want anything? No ma'am, I ain't said nothin' like that. Did you hear me make one little re-quest?

CHERRY: Naw, but . . .

CLYDE: And you wonder why I wanna get from 'round here. People don't know how to be friendly, that's why.

CHERRY: Friendly? Just don't be eyeing that bottle and I'll be friendly. Mrs. Fair gave me that to cook with for special dress-up times. It was a Christmas present. Just keep your paws off!

CLYDE: Well, I'll be. Ain't you got hell in you this day?

CHERRY: Hail Mary full of Graces!

CLYDE: Hail who? Oh, you talkin' some of that Hoodoo again?

CHERRY: It ain't Hoodoo. It's called religion.

CLYDE: Shoot! You don't got to get all uppity. Don't act like that with me. I known you since you was knee high to a grasshopper and loud as a cricket in the moonlight.

CHERRY [*cracking eggs into a bowl*]: Clyde, you on my last nerve.

CLYDE: You heard me.

CHERRY: Ain't nobody gettin' into all that with you. I got too much on my mind. Holy Mary! Clyde, you done made me forget how many eggs I done put in there!

CLYDE: I'm sorry. I just thought that you'd enjoy some company.

CHERRY [*counting egg shells*]: Oomph!

CLYDE: Three.

CHERRY: What?

CLYDE: You put in three eggs.

CHERRY: Thanks.

CLYDE: Do you mind if I have me a glass of water? This heat's 'bout to drive me mad.

CHERRY [*grabbing a pitcher of water and placing it on the table.*]: Here. Pour it yourself.

CLYDE: Well, I will do just that. Yes, ma'am. Ain't nothin' like the tears of God to quench a man's thirst.

CHERRY: Tears of God. That sounds kinda sad.

CLYDE: Maybe. I figure he gots to be a little sad to see how people have messed up his creation.

CHERRY: That does make sense. [*Beat*] How's your Uncle Titus?

CLYDE: Fine, just fine. He's waiting on a letter from Uncle Giles. He oughta be in Denver 'round 'bout now.

CHERRY [*to herself in amazement*]: Denver!

CLYDE: Yeah, must have passed the Rockies. Seem like it didn't take 'um no time.

CHERRY: So far from here. Denver. Even the name sounds cold.

CLYDE: Cold or not, I'm going next! Ridin' 'long with the Raymond family. [*Strutting around the kitchen, then pulling a photo from his pocket*] Here's a picture Uncle Giles gave me before he left. That's my cousin Tommy and his friend out there in California. They got jobs on the docks. They gonna get Giles one once he get there.

CHERRY: You don't say. [*Looking at the picture*] So you goin' next? For true?

CLYDE: Yeah, the women needs me out there. Heard it's ten womens to every man. I'm just tryin' to do my patriotic duty!

CHERRY [*laughs*]: You crazy! [*Nicer*] How many people going with y'all?

CLYDE: I ain't too sure. I'll have to set down with Mr. Raymond and see about our arrangements.

CHERRY: You really goin' to California?

CLYDE: Sure 'nough. I wasted too much time in this old dusty place. It's too small for me. I aim to be a mighty man. Folks around here don't take to men like me being mighty.

CHERRY [*thoughtful silence*]: You want some more water?

CLYDE [*pointing to sherry bottle*]: Well . . . do you mind if I just get a taste of that?

CHERRY: You done gone from God's tears to the devil's spit! I don't know what to do with you. No, you cain't!

CLYDE: Come on now, that white lady give you somethin' like that and you won't share it? Cherry, I'm practically family! Come on.

CHERRY: No.

CLYDE: Let me just get myself a 'lil taste.

CHERRY: Clyde!

CLYDE: Don't get all fussy. Calm yourself. You 'bout to wake Mother Henry.

CHERRY: Yeah, and you'll be the one that has to answer to her—not me.

CLYDE: Come on now . . .

CHERRY: Go on and take a swig if you so parched. Instead of worrying about your thirst, you need to be worried 'bout your soul. You need to be thinkin' 'bout gettin' to that revival. You need to be worried about drinkin' from the fountain of Jesus.

CLYDE: I ain't worried about that bottle, girl. That ain't what I'm here for. Please know, I may not sit on the pews of True Vine every Sunday, but

I do feel that God speaks to me. All the time. He tells me what I need to do. Yes, he speaks to me.

CHERRY: Clyde?

CLYDE: Miss?

CHERRY: Get on out of here so I can finish my bakin'.

CLYDE: I'm not in your way.

[CLYDE *gazes at* CHERRY *while she bakes, smiles, then tips his hat.*]

But I'll go. Just remember, you gonna miss me when I'm gone. See you at the revival. So long, Miss Cherry Pie.

[CLYDE *walks out of the kitchen.* CHERRY *continues baking and begins to hum.*]

SCENE 4. DREAMING ON A DREAM

[MA HENRY'*s porch later that afternoon. A basket of laundry rests on the porch.* MA HENRY *is sitting in a rocking chair sewing a quilt.* CHERRY *enters and begins folding clothes.*]

CHERRY: That's pretty! Ma, did you find that thread you like in the basket?

MA HENRY: I ain't worried about that thread, baby. Lose one thread and there will always be another. Looks like rain comin'. Them pies still coolin' out on the windowsill?

CHERRY: Yes, ma'am. Pecan, sweet potato, and apple.

MA HENRY: I ain't nevah heard of nothin' like that before. You musta got that way of coolin' ya pies from Mrs. Fair. That sure sound like some white idears. Don't you know that ants will crawl all over your sweets? Anybody who got sense know that.

CHERRY: All God's creatures deserve to live and enjoy them some sweetness.

MA HENRY: Not on my windowsill! [*Beat*] Make sure you fold those towels straight now, last time you left a mess in my cupboard.

CHERRY: Yes, ma'am. Ma Henry, you ever thought about leavin' Monroe?

MA HENRY: When I was a young girl I reckon I had all kind of foolish thoughts. Why? You fixin' your mind on leavin'? Where you gonna go? Neptune?

CHERRY: I—well, I been thinkin' 'bout California. [*Dreamily*] I'd like to see the ocean.

MA HENRY: Cherry, tell me what all this is about?

CHERRY: Maybe I can get a job there, baking pies at one of those fancy restaurants where all the movie stars go. 'Member that picture about the lady with the restaurant?

MA HENRY: That Crawford lady's movie?

CHERRY: Yes! *Mildred Pierce.*

MA HENRY: Stop the silly talk. Wait. Ain't Clyde been talkin' 'bout going to California too?

CHERRY: I ain't worried 'bout what he's talkin' 'bout. I'm makin' my own plans.

MA HENRY: The movie pictures are the movie pictures. You need to put your feet on the ground in this life. I don't want to hear this madness. I don't want to hear about no ocean and no fancy shops.

CHERRY: Please don't be upset with me. I don't mean no disrespect. I was just thinking about what it would be like to do something that folks would talk about for all time. "Did you hear about Cherry Henry? She got her own pie restaurant in California." Don't you wanna brag about me to all the church mothers at True Vine, Ma Henry?

MA HENRY: Girl, I don't understand what's got into you but you needs to pray for the Lord to take it off ya. Clyde James wanna drag you off with him then he better come in here and ask for your hand like he knows he oughta.

CHERRY: I don't want to be bothered with that silly ole' Clyde. Don't nobody need to do nothin' but let me go.

[CLYDE *walks up*; CHERRY *and* MA HENRY *are both quiet for a beat.*]

MA HENRY [*under her breath*]: Speak of the devil and he will appear.

CLYDE: Good afternoon, Ma Henry, Miss Cherry. How y'all doin'? [*Nobody responds.*]

MA HENRY AND CHERRY [*stoically, in unison*]: Fine.

CLYDE: All right. Well, I come by for those pies for the revival. Sister Betty said she wanted to set up the tent early.

MA HENRY: They ought to be cooled off by now. Got to be careful about things being too hot. You just might burn yourself.

[CHERRY *hurries into the house. Lights down.*]

SCENE 5. REVIVAL

[*Evening outside the revival tent. Sounds of the preacher, choir, and congregation rise and fall during the scene.* CHERRY *is standing at the flap handing out programs and fans herself. She peeks in the tent on occasion to hear the sermon and then takes notice of* CLYDE *and* SEYMOUR *as they approach.*]

CLYDE: Well, good evening, pretty lady!

SEYMOUR: Hey, Miss Cherry! Nice to see you this evenin'.

CHERRY: Evenin,' y'all. [*She hands them both programs.*]

CLYDE [*to* SEYMOUR]: Seymour, you sly possum! I had no idea that you was also acquainted with the prettiest girl in Monroe, Miss Cherry Henry.

SEYMOUR: Indeed I am. But I'm no possum, sir! I'm a sly fox 'cause I don't play dead! How are you tonight, Miss Cherry?

CHERRY: I'm just fine, Seymour. Thanks for your inquiry. How are you?

SEYMOUR: I'm quite well and ready to receive the word. As they say, "This is the day the Lord has made. Let us rejoice and be glad in it."

CLYDE: Ain't you gonna ask me how I'm doin', Miss Cherry?

CHERRY: No, I won't, Clyde, because you probably up to no good—even at a revival!

SEYMOUR: Well, I ain't gettin' in no trouble. I don't court trouble at all. I'm too grown for that. You bake any pies lately, Miss Cherry?

CHERRY: I surely have.

SEYMOUR: I do hope I get a chance to partake of one of your masterpieces. I'd consider it an honor.

CHERRY: If you mean get a slice of pie, Seymour, then why don't you go on over to Sister Tolliver's table? She selling my pies over there for twenty-five cents a slice.

CLYDE: She selling slices of your pecan pie too? Seeing that I helped by bringing you those fresh pecans I oughta be able to get me a slice for free—

SEYMOUR: Well, I'll buy me a whole pie. I believe they worth every penny! A man would be blessed to have your pies to come home to every night. A smart man would see that.

CHERRY: I don't know too many of them. Besides, not all girls are looking forward to a man coming home hungry every night. Some of us got different dreams.

CLYDE: And some of us got big dreams.

SEYMOUR: We all got dreams. Big and small and they all matter to God.

CHERRY: Enough about dreams for tonight. Y'all goin' in? Or you think God gonna tap you on the shoulder and bless you out here?

CLYDE: Shoot! I feel mighty good just bein' on the outside. I don't want to ruin things by running up in there too fast.

SEYMOUR: Well, Miss Cherry, I'm not like this rascal! I come to hear the good Reverend Barker. It looks like Clyde found the miracle he came here for.

CHERRY: Is that right?

SEYMOUR: Yes, it appears so. That's all right. There's a few more of God's angels in the tent to stir a man's soul. This tent is pitched on hallowed ground tonight. Let me get my blessing. Y'all have a nice evenin'.

[SEYMOUR *enters the tent.*]

CHERRY: Night.

[CHERRY *turns toward* CLYDE.]

CLYDE: You look pretty, Cherry.

CHERRY: Thank you, Clyde. It's a new dress. Sewed it myself. Well, don't look like any more people are coming tonight. I better get inside—

CLYDE: Sure is a nice night for a stroll 'round Jupiter Pond.

CHERRY: A stroll? You been drinkin', Clyde?

CLYDE: I been drinkin' all night! I'm drunk off the moon. I'm down right sloshed off the smell of this old dirt and I can't see straight 'cause the sounds of angels are in my ears. You oughta take a drink yourself sometime.

CHERRY [*laughing*]: Me? Drink? I ain't nevah had none of that.

CLYDE: Why not? It ain't done me no harm.

CHERRY: I'm a very important person. Drinking the moon don't fit. Look at you, Clyde. I don't know anybody else who would show his face at a revival nearly ready to pass out. You better not let Reverend Barker find you like this. He'll put you in the pulpit as an example of how to not be a child of God.

CLYDE: Cherry, let's get out of here. I need to talk to you. I gots some things to say.

CHERRY: If you in such a hurry why don't we talk now, right here?

CLYDE: All right. [*Pause*] It's just that I'm hopin' to leave real soon. The Raymonds and them are pushing up they run out west. They got a sick cousin out there. If I'm leavin' with them then I gotta leave next week. Not much time for—

CHERRY: What you sayin'? What about your job?

CLYDE: That ain't no reason to stay. Old man Peterson lookin' for somebody to put chains on. Even with the war over they still sayin' they can't pay us regular. You can't fight them. Look at what happened to Jefferson—

CHERRY: I don't know nothin' 'bout that.

CLYDE: You do. You just don't want to see it. [*Beat*] They makin' money hand over fist at the shipyards in San Francisco. I'm going after mine too.

CHERRY: San Francisco? The city with the golden bridge?

CLYDE: Yep! They makin' money, Cherry. Got themselves some of that gold.

CHERRY: What else they say?

CLYDE: That it's nice. White folks don't bother you. Negroes even own a few little things.

CHERRY: This is my home. This is where I grew up. It's where my grandma is. Where all my people are buried.

CLYDE: Well, I just don't want to rush myself into the grave. I want to see more of the world. If I die it will be with a smile on my face.

CHERRY [*annoyed*]: Well good for you. Thanks for tellin' me. I don't feel so well. I best be gettin' back home.

CLYDE: I'm headin' that way. I'll help you carry your pans on over to the house.

CHERRY: I don't need no help!

CLYDE: If you slow down a minute. I gots somethin' to ask.

CHERRY: Well . . .

CLYDE: A man 'round here has plenty to walk through. I ain't plannin' on raisin' no kids in Monroe, Cherry.

CHERRY: Yeah? What's that got to do with me?

CLYDE: If you listen a minute you'll find out. [*Gathers his nerve*] I know you want things for yourself too.

CHERRY: What you know about what I want? That's between me and God.

CLYDE: Are you set on this place? Do you plan to stay with Ma Henry for the rest of your life?

CHERRY: Why you worried 'bout that?

CLYDE: You oughta come on and go with us.

CHERRY: What you mean?

CLYDE: Yeah, let's ride out to the West. Ain't no Indians to be afraid of no more!

CHERRY: I ain't worried 'bout no Indians. I can't believe—

[MA HENRY *comes out of the tent, sees* CLYDE *and* CHERRY *and walks over to them.*]

MA HENRY: What y'all doin' out here?

CLYDE: Evenin', Mrs. Henry. I'm—

MA HENRY: Prayin' in the wrong place. You need to get on in there. Reverend Barker blessin' everything he see.

CHERRY: Did you enjoy the choir, Ma?

MA HENRY: They was too loud for me. [*To* CLYDE] I suggest you go on in while they got seats left near the front. They say, the closer to Jesus—

CLYDE AND CHERRY [*in unison*]: Yes, ma'am.

MA HENRY: Well, I'm tired and fixin' to head home. [*To* CHERRY] You comin' or going, girl?

CHERRY: I'll be 'round in a bit. Night, Ma.

MA HENRY: Best make it quick.

CHERRY: Yes, ma'am.

MA HENRY: Night. [*Takes a long look at* CLYDE.]

CLYDE: Evenin', ma'am.

[MA HENRY *departs. To* CHERRY]

Now you ain't gonna rush home and leave me by my lonesome?

CHERRY [*sitting down on the bench in front of the tent*]: You pressurin' me. I just ain't sure how I'm being led. You was friends with Jefferson. Seems like you always been around as long as I can remember, but running off with you across the whole America? Besides . . .

CLYDE: What? You ain't still stuck on Jimmy Tyler! You think he's gonna marry you and set up shop around here? He ain't brave enough to fight a fly. That fool—

CHERRY: Hush, it ain't even 'bout him.

CLYDE: Then who? What would keep you here? Don't you have dreams of your own?

CHERRY: I don't think you'll understand. I don't know if I should tell you this.

CLYDE: I asked you to come with me out to California, you can tell me anything.

CHERRY: Well, the night we lost Jefferson . . . I had what you call a vision.

CLYDE: What you mean?

CHERRY: Mary the Virgin came to me in my sleep.

CLYDE: What? You mean Jesus's mama?

CHERRY: Yes, Mary, beautiful as can be. Us both virgins.

CLYDE: Is that right? Well now, that's quite a dream.

CHERRY: But this wasn't no dream—it was a vision.

CLYDE: All right. Tell me about it.

CHERRY: I remember her hair in long braids all over her head. Thickest plaits I ever done seen. It was black and she smelled like cinnamon—dusty and brown. Yeah, she was brown too, Mary.

CLYDE: Is that right? Did she say something or did she just look at ya?

CHERRY: She explained it all to me. She said I was chosen. Mary said that I was picked to give birth to the next child for the Lord. Me, Cherry.

CLYDE: You, of all the faithful in Louisiana?

CHERRY: Me. [*Pause*] That night Mary spoke to me in a singing rhythm full of rejoicing—but she was serious too. She said "Cherry, don't ever forget this is an honor, being chosen to do God's work means living up to his word." I never did forget that. I didn't exactly know what she meant, but I woke up the next morning with such a peaceful feelin'.

CLYDE: I'll be! Wasn't you scared? I would have been.

CHERRY: Oh, I was very afraid, but I knew then that I had responsibilities. Big ones. That vision changed my life. [*Pause*] Clyde, I don't think I can go with you to California.

CLYDE: Fine! You stay here with your visions. You think you're the only one that got visitors in the night? I got nightmares chasing me, girl! You don't want to know what haints come to me in the dark when I'm all alone. [*Beat*] I don't want to stay here dancing with those visions.

CHERRY: You're afraid just like me.

CLYDE: Maybe, but you best believe that I'm not afraid of chasing my dreams. I'm on the next thing out of here that's running.

CHERRY [*grabbing his arm*]: Clyde, I knew you wouldn't understand—

CLYDE: No, I don't understand nothin' 'bout this place!

[CLYDE *storms off stage right.*]

CHERRY [*in a trancelike voice, while ethereal light bathes over her*]: I am the conduit between earth, this soil of Monroe, Louisiana, and the divine. Me, Cherry Louise Henry. Second Mother of the Second Coming.

[CLYDE *returns. Stands looking at* CHERRY. *He extends his hand. Lights down.*]

SCENE 6. THUNDER

[MA HENRY'*s house at dawn after a terrible storm the night of the revival.* MA HENRY *is sitting at the kitchen table with a cup of tea. She's wearing a nightgown and slippers, and her hair is wrapped up in a scarf.* CHERRY *walks into the kitchen. She's noticeably startled by* MA HENRY'*s presence, but regains her composure and tries to act at ease.*]

CHERRY: Ma!

MA HENRY: Girl, I'm fit to be tied! I been waitin' on you.

CHERRY: I'm sorry, Mother Henry.

MA HENRY: You betta be sorry—

CHERRY: Yes, ma'am. You really shouldn't be out of bed. Fall almost set in. It startin' to get mighty cool at night. You gonna catch your death—

MA HENRY: Don't fret 'bout where I oughta be. I've lived plenty long. I'm worried 'bout how you living!

CHERRY: I'm just saying that storm went on somethin' awful—like the world was 'bout to come to an end.

MA HENRY: Yeah, that sky was howlin' mighty loud. You think a young lady oughta be out in sumpin' like that? It ain't right, Cherry Louise Henry—it's nearly daylight out there. That ain't no way for a grandbaby of mine to be carryin' on. Storm or not, you know these roads ain't no place to be for a Colored girl alone. No tellin' what might happen.

CHERRY: I'm real sorry, Ma. The revival went on and folks got to talkin' and . . . You want some more tea?

MA HENRY: No, I don't want no more tea. [*Silence.*]

CHERRY: Don't you worry though, I wasn't up to nothin' bad. So you don't need to worry 'bout that. [*Walks to the stove to put on the teakettle.*]

MA HENRY: I just need you to tell me where you went after the revival, Cherry. It don't make no sense for you to be out at this hour of the mornin' and with your Sunday outfit on too.

CHERRY: Well, it's kinda strange. I know you gonna think—

MA HENRY: If you don't fix your mouth to talk to me I'ma getta switch out of that yard and help you think straight. You ain't too old for that. I know it and you do too. Where you been, Cherry?

CHERRY: Talkin' to Clyde, ma'am. Clyde James.

MA HENRY: What! It's almost dawn and you tellin' me you was just up *talkin'* to that boy?

CHERRY: Yes, Ma Henry. I act just the way you raised me.

MA HENRY: So, I guess that baby you carryin' his?

CHERRY: What?

MA HENRY: Don't fix your lips to lie to me. Is it his?

CHERRY: No, ma'am! How did you know I was even gonna have a baby?

MA HENRY: I hear you been over to the doctor's. You think white folks think twice about a keepin' a Colored girl's secrets?

CHERRY: I—

MA HENRY: I've been on this here earth for many years. I can't believe you tryin' to tell me that baby don't belong to Clyde James!

CHERRY: But, ma'am, it ain't his.

MA HENRY: Then whose is it?

CHERRY [*after a pause*]: I cain't explain.

MA HENRY: Hmph. I can! I know it like I know the face of my daddy. I'll tear that boy's hide apart when I sees him again. Ain't worth the dirt on his overalls. What kinda husband he gonna be? What kinda daddy? He can barely keep a job at Peterson's. Girl, I don't know what's wrong with you!

CHERRY: Maybe I'm as loony as everybody thinks I am.

MA HENRY: I tell you what! You havin' a child with that triflin' James boy proves you out of your mind!

CHERRY [*starts to pray silently*]: I just wish you'd stop.

MA HENRY: What? You ain't gonna tell me you're in love with that fool?

CHERRY: No! I don't love anybody but Jesus.

MA HENRY: Lord knows I've tried to keep you on a righteous path but now you out here carrying on like a—

CHERRY: This baby ain't from a man; it's God's!

MA HENRY: Stop!

CHERRY: Mary came to me in a vision and—

MA HENRY [*rising in anger*]: You hush your mouth! Blasphemy is a sin to go along with all your others. Mary had herself a husband, if you know your Bible then you know that. Ain't no Joseph been 'round this house, at least as far as I seen! Mark my words, if he is the father then you better have that boy or somebody upstanding marry you. [*Under her breath*] Fool out here ruining my grandbaby! I ought to take a shotgun to him myself.

CHERRY: It's not his baby. It's not his baby!

MA HENRY: I don't care what you say! You might as well marry that boy so that the child will at least have a father. I guess you two could have this house after I'm gone. Least that way the child won't be . . . won't be a—

CHERRY: What Ma Henry? A bastard? Is that what you gonna call your great grand? If he is a bastard than he ain't no more of a bastard than Jesus himself!

[MA HENRY *slaps her face.*]

MA HENRY: I won't hear that talk in this house! Don't speak that blasphemous talk in the house that your father, a man of God, built with his own hands. Girl I'll—

CHERRY [*stunned, holding her cheek.*]: So, I'll marry him! I'll marry Clyde! Will you be happy then? Will you give my leaving a blessing?

MA HENRY: Happy? I gave up on happy a long time ago. [*Sitting down, devastated*] You leaving?

CHERRY: He is asking me to go to California with him.

MA HENRY: Is that a marriage proposal?

CHERRY: No, Ma.

MA HENRY: Of course he ain't proposing! [*Pause*] When you due?

CHERRY: It will come in March I think. A spring baby. A new day in California, USA. [*Wistfully*] Praise God, Holy Mary, a new season.

MA HENRY: I don't know about Mary. I just want you safe. What if folks don't like you out there? They ain't gonna know ya. I'd rather stay where I know folk and folk know me. You know what to expect and how to act and what the spring will be like.

CHERRY: Ma! I want this baby to know something different. We can learn together 'bout this new world.

MA HENRY: Seems to me the mother oughta know more than the child.

CHERRY: Jefferson would understand if he was alive.

MA HENRY: Jefferson would never walk off on the family. And if he knew somebody sniffed after his sister he would have had something to say about it.

CHERRY: Well, that ain't somethin' he will ever get a chance to do again!

MA HENRY [*sucking her teeth in disgust*]: Hmph. [*Angry pause*] 'Bout to get my pressure up. Don't believe I'm sitting here this time of the morning fussin' with you.

CHERRY: I'm sorry.

MA HENRY: I'm gonna lay down.

[MA HENRY *walks to her bedroom.* CHERRY *enters the house and lights a candle that sits next to a black-and-white 8 × 10 photograph of a dignified older black couple.* CHERRY *touches the crucifix she's wearing around her neck, then kisses the photograph. She takes off her shoes and gets down on her knees and begins an awkward Catholic-style prayer session, making the sign of the cross—but in the wrong direction. During the prayer an angelic light washes over* CHERRY. *The prayer and light transform her.*]

CHERRY: Dear Mary, Jesus, and God too. Please y'all, help me to find my way out of this place. Allow me to do your will. Teach me to live my life as a tribute to your divine power and grace.

I want to live near the ocean. I want to see a new world full of beauty and peace.

Please Lord, I mean—Hail Mary—let me get myself to California safe. I don't want this child you gave me to ever know life like this—dirt and no pretty things. Guide me to California where nobody hurts you 'cause you Colored and all the people shops in big stores. Amen.

[CHERRY *does her version of the sign of the cross and blows out the candle. Lights fade out. The same choir of humming voices that opened the play returns. Then silence.*]

ACT 2. TRAVELING LIGHT

SCENE 1. KISSIN' COUSINS

[*Afternoon, two days later.* MA HENRY *is sitting at the kitchen table talking with* VIOLA. *They are having a good time laughing and catching up on the local gossip.* CHERRY *comes in with a bag of hand-me-down clothes from Mrs. Fair. She stops when she sees* VIOLA. *She begins to prepare for the evening meal.*]

VIOLA [*fanning herself*]: And it's so hot! Whew!

MA HENRY: Hush, girl. You ain't gonna melt none.

VIOLA: My goodness, I've nearly forgotten about all these ants down here. They're sure biting today! [*Slaps away pests.*]

MA HENRY: So good to finally have you home. How long you plan to be 'round this time?

VIOLA: I'm not sure, Ma Henry. You trying to get rid of me?

MA HENRY: No such thing. I just got to set my heart just right.

VIOLA: Well, I'm here now, and since I'm in town I need to go over to True Vine and see Sister Mabel. She's been after me to sing a solo at Sunday service and I aim to do just that. [*Looking at her reflection in the window and fixing her hair*] Maybe I'll get on that train come Wednesday. That will give me a chance to get settled before my shift—I mean before I need to get to the office on Monday.

MA HENRY: That ain't much time, that's barely a week. It sure is quiet when you're gone. [*Glancing toward the kitchen*] Did that Cherry sneak in here and not speak? [*To* CHERRY] Cherry! Girl, come and see what done rolled in with the wind!

CHERRY [*shyly entering from the kitchen, with towel in hand*]: Hello, Vi.

VIOLA [*standing up to give her a Hollywood kiss and hug*]: Sugar! Look at you! You look wonderful. Did you make that dress yourself? [*To* MA HENRY] I really do miss lookin' at homemade dresses. [*Touching the hem of* CHERRY*'s dress*] All these store bought things don't fit as snug you know.

MA HENRY: If you put some more meat on your bones you'd fill 'em out just fine.

VIOLA: Cherry sure isn't havin' any trouble fillin' out her wardrobe. You puttin' on weight, cousin?

CHERRY: No!

MA HENRY: Oh she's fine. Cherry, get this skinny thing a piece of that apple pie. She makes it just like her mama did. That crust is as flaky and buttery as the sun is hot.

CHERRY: We out of apple pie, Ma. You want some peach cobbler, Vi?

VIOLA: Peach cobbler? I haven't eaten that since the last time I was down here. Not my favorite but I'll go on and have some cobbler. And pour me a tall glass of milk from that sweet cow Tillie, if it's no trouble.

CHERRY [*going to the kitchen for milk*]: I don't milk no cows anymore. We get our milk delivered, Vi.

VIOLA: Hmm. Well, I'll be.

MA HENRY [*as* CHERRY *leaves for the kitchen*]: She's been such a big help now with everyone else passed on or moved away.

VIOLA: Well, not everybody is made for this place. I wish I had the will, the strength, and the talent for it.

MA HENRY: Vi, you got more to do in this life than milk Tillie and have babies. How's that learnin' goin'?

VIOLA: Chicago is a lovely town. I had to stop school for a while because I was gettin' so much work. I just didn't have time. I read when I can, books by Shakespeare and poetry by Donne. Even some Negro writers like Richard Wright. He wrote a whole entire book about the South Side of Chicago.

MA HENRY: South Side?

VIOLA: That's where the Colored folks live.

MA HENRY: That sure sound fancy. I'd like to see somethin' nice like that one day.

VIOLA: I'll send you a copy of the book as soon as I get home.

[CHERRY *enters with cobbler and a tall glass of milk and places them before* VIOLA.]

MA HENRY: That will be nice. Cherry talkin' 'bout leavin' here too, Vi. Won't nobody be here after a while.

VIOLA: Where you off to, Miss Cherry? You coming to the Windy City too?

CHERRY: Where's the windy city?

VIOLA: It's what us locals call Chicago. It's kind of a pet name.

MA HENRY: Go on and tell your cousin where you're off to—and tell her with who!

CHERRY [*barely audible*]: I'm thinkin' 'bout goin' out to California. Clyde said he gonna take me. But—

VIOLA: Who? Not that handsome Clyde James? He takin' my little ole cousin Cherry away from Monroe? Well, I'll be.

CHERRY: We goin' to ride with the Raymond family. This time they takin' two whole carloads out West. They leaving soon.

VIOLA: Yeah, soon as one of the Raymonds get to town they drag somebody else off with them. They like a family full of Harriet Tubmans!

[VIOLA *laughs.*]

MA HENRY: So did that boy Giles ever go?

CHERRY: Sure did. On that last trip. Clyde said they oughta be in California soon. They don't stop for nothin' but petrol and food. [*Excitedly*] Im'a pack us some sandwiches for us so when we go we don't haveta stop for nothin' but Ethyl.

VIOLA [*fanning herself*]: Oh my! That don't sound very civilized. My legs would get so cramped. I guess I'm used to something different because I be ridin' in these trains. I love eating my meals in the dining car with a pretty white linen napkin and shiny silverware. Honey, I would have to stop and jump out of that automobile just to get my composure.

CHERRY: Composure? I don't think we need none of that.

VIOLA: That don't mean . . . everybody needs composure, sugar. It means time to gather your nerves. [*Tasting the cobbler*] Um. What will you and Clyde be up to in California?

MA HENRY [*to* CHERRY]: What did he tell you?

CHERRY: Well, he's gonna get a good job and—

VIOLA [*slapping her arm and rubbing an insect bite*]: If it ain't the ants it's these vicious mosquitoes! I don't know how y'all deal with it. I can't stand it anymore.

MA HENRY: Must be nice and pretty all the time in Chicago.

VIOLA: It's simply gorgeous—until the winter hits and the Hawk makes its appearance.

CHERRY: What's the Hawk?

VIOLA: The Chicago wind. It's cold! And meaner than a hurricane 'cause it cuts through your clothes and don't disappear after the storm is over.

MA HENRY: Do y'all get a lot of snow?

VIOLA: Sometimes two or three feet in a day!

CHERRY: That sounds awful! I heard in California they don't even got no winter—just always spring.

MA HENRY: That don't sound normal to me.

VIOLA: Everywhere got seasons, sweetie.

CHERRY: Not California!

MA HENRY: Betty Raymond wrote her folks and say it do rain and everythin'. And what about them earthquakes? That thing in 1906 was a monster. [*Shaking her head*] Like I said, that place don't sound quite right to me.

VIOLA: And it's really far, Cherry. Why don't y'all come up to the Windy City instead? I'm sure I could even find you a job.

MA HENRY: That do make more sense.

VIOLA: I'm headin' back early next week and you could just jump on the train with me and—

CHERRY: No! Me and Clyde goin' to California—that's it!

VIOLA: Oh! So you marrying Clyde?

MA HENRY: That's what we all waitin' to hear.

VIOLA: Things do change. Leave town for a little while and—

CHERRY: I'm used to having him around. Seem like he was always here with Jefferson. He's always been my friend too.

VIOLA: Friend? [*Laughing*] Sugar, I have plenty of real special friends in Chicago, but I don't marry them.

MA HENRY: Viola, when are you thinkin' on marryin'?

VIOLA: Not for a while, Ma. I'm still gettin' settled in Chicago. [*Beat*] What do you think I should sing on Sunday, Cherry?

CHERRY: I don't know.

MA HENRY: Oh baby, you always do a good job with "Precious Lord." I hope you sing that when they lay these old bones to rest.

VIOLA: Oh, Ma!

CHERRY: Don't you talk like that. We have plenty of years before that day comes.

VIOLA: Yes, Ma. We know you've got a long road still ahead. I'm not singing no funeral song on Sunday. Maybe I'll sing "Strange Things Happening Everyday."

MA HENRY: I'm sure the church will be grateful for whatever you bless us with.

CHERRY: You want some more pie, Ma? I'll fetch you a nice piece of apple pie.

MA HENRY: That sounds real good, baby.

VIOLA: Wait a minute. I thought you didn't have no more apple pie.

CHERRY: I musta forgot about that one little piece. You know how silly I can be! Sorry, cousin.

[CHERRY *brings a slice of apple pie to* MA HENRY. CHERRY *and* VIOLA *stare at one another.*]

MA HENRY [*grabbing their hands and closing her eyes*]: Thank you, Jesus, for bringing my two sweet grandbabies here with me. My God sure is a gracious God.

CHERRY: Yes, Ma. He sure 'nuff is.

VIOLA: He certainly is.

[VIOLA *takes a bite of* MA HENRY*'s slice of apple pie while still staring at* CHERRY.]

[*Lights fade to black.*]

SCENE 2. TALKING TO DEATH

[*That same evening, inside the neighborhood bar.* CLYDE *dances to a tune on the jukebox (maybe Louis Jordan's "Choo Choo Ch'Boogie"). He stops, then sits on a stool at the bar.* SEYMOUR *is drying glasses.*]

CLYDE [*grabbing a handful of peanuts*]: Seymour, pour me another finger of that gin.

SEYMOUR: Yes, sir!

CLYDE: These white folks 'round here 'bout ta drive me out of my head.

SEYMOUR: You talkin' 'bout Petersons?

CLYDE: Yup. It ain't just them though. You heard about them boys that got hung out in that field in Natchez?

SEYMOUR: I heard. Damn shame.

CLYDE: But Mississippi ain't got nothing on us. I heard what they did to that family in Lake Charles. Nobody met their maker but . . . [*Sighing*] I'm 'bout sick of this place.

SEYMOUR: Well, you off to California soon enough. Ain't got to be sick no more.

CLYDE: You right.

SEYMOUR: Heading way on the other side of the country. That's a long way from home, youngin. A long way.

CLYDE: I can't get far enough away from here.

SEYMOUR: Is that right? You sound like a man on a mission. Let me not get in your way. You ain't gonna miss Monroe at all?

CLYDE: Well, there is one place I'll miss.

SEYMOUR: Where is that?

CLYDE: Out in the grove 'round Jupiter pond.

SEYMOUR: Yeah, it's quiet there. Nice piece of land.

CLYDE: Man that big rock out there, ain't nothin' like the feelin' of that rock under me. I wouldn't mind livin' somewhere like that for all my days.

SEYMOUR: So you ready to find you another rock way out there in California?

CLYDE: No need to waste time living where they don't want me, where they hangin' folks. That boy they killed out in Minden last month got his private parts to eat for all eternity. What sense that make?

SEYMOUR: No sense at all. But my daddy told me long ago, if you looking for sense in this world then you looking in the wrong place. You gotta look for sense inside you. Carry that with you on every road you travel.

CLYDE [*drinking a shot of gin in one gulp*]: Yes, sir. Sense or no sense, this place ain't for me. I'll see California before this year ends. I'm gonna make me a way to see that land of gold and fruit. I'm tired of workin' like a dog, livin' like a slave, and hidin' like a fool . . . wanna live like a man.

SEYMOUR: Go on, man! Tell it.

CLYDE: Tired of bowing my head down to every cracker thinkin' of cookin' himself a nigga.

SEYMOUR [*after a pause*]: What it smell like, Clyde?

CLYDE: You know Saturday and girls fryin' they hair? Pressin' it smells like smoke with a little bit of dust. You know the smell of burnt hair . . . pressed way too close to the scalp?

SEYMOUR: You the one who cut him down then?

CLYDE: Yeah. [*Pause*] Heaviest load I ever carried. After that I stayed drunk goin' on a week. Maybe two. Every morning I woke up I just turned to that bottle in the bed with me, took a swig and another wink. Was this close to being fired. I keep thinking over and over, if only I had been there in time I woulda—

SEYMOUR: Then who would have cut you down?

CLYDE: Give me another shot.

SEYMOUR [*pouring another shot, then pushing the glass over to* CLYDE]: This ought to do you nice.

CLYDE: Appreciate it.

SEYMOUR: You all right?

CLYDE: You know I've been thinking of chopping down that tree. I never want to see those branches again.

SEYMOUR [*drying glasses*]: Don't own it. Can't cut it.

CLYDE: Guess they got me there huh?

SEYMOUR: They got us more ways than that. [*Pause*] Besides, the trees are innocent. Those old trees are beautiful. They've seen all kinds of fruit and watched plenty of mischief. The trees of Monroe watched over my papa when he met my mama at a church picnic. I climbed those same trees when I was a boy. Now I have chopped off a few dead limbs when I needed to build a fire for a cold winter night, but it ain't right to cut a whole tree down.

CLYDE: How you think you gonna die, Seymour? Ever think about that?

SEYMOUR: Can't say I do. Got other things to keep my mind occupied.

[SEYMOUR *pours another drink for* CLYDE *and then pours one for himself.*]

CLYDE: Listen, this is one man who ain't gonna be cooked like stew for the coffin. [*Beat*] From what I understand you meet your maker the same way you leave here. So if you hit the dusty road to hell without your head? Ichabod Crane you is forever. Shit! I wanna look good in my afterlife. When I gotta go it's gonna be in grand style. Just like a king. I don't know what you're thinkin'—but I'm not going to die like that. No sir, gotta go out like an old English king.

SEYMOUR: Here! Here! Hail, King Clyde James.

[*Both men toast the sentiment.*]

[*Lights down.*]

SCENE 3. RISING STAR

[*Sunday afternoon.* MA HENRY, VIOLA, CHERRY, *and* CLYDE *walk to the porch after church.* CLYDE *examines the railing and then starts to oil the screen door hinges.*]

MA HENRY: Folks sure were happy to have you back. The choir ain't sounded that good in a long while.

VIOLA [*taking off her hat*]: It feels good to be home. I love seeing everyone all dressed up in their finest.

MA HENRY [*sitting down in her rocker*]: Everybody did look good this morning.

VIOLA: Well, I tell you, the men in Chicago dress so fine. You really oughta see them, Ma Henry. Pretty clothes, sharp shoes—

MA HENRY: A Christian woman shouldn' have too many fine dressin' men 'round if you ask me. Unless one of them men is a husband type of man.

CLYDE: What do a real man need with pretty clothes?

MA HENRY: What you know about real men, Clyde James?

VIOLA: Whew! Ma Henry, don't bust his chops.

MA HENRY [*under her breath*]: Hmm. He lucky I don't bust more than that.

CHERRY: Anybody want a piece of pound cake?

MA HENRY: Yes, sweetheart, bring Ma a great big ole piece. I want to eat right out here on the porch like we use to when you and Vi was little bitty girls.

VIOLA: Cousin, I'd love to taste more of your baking. You sure do know your way around a kitchen, sugar. I'd love to be like Mrs. Fair one day—rich enough to have someone like you to cook and clean for me.

CLYDE: If you got enough for me I'd sure be obliged.

CHERRY [*on her way to the kitchen*]: Coming right up.

CLYDE [*loudly to nobody in particular*]: I'm gonna get me an automobile. I wants me an Oldsmobile or maybe even a Cadillac.

VIOLA: My friend Charles has a red Cadillac convertible. [*Strolling around the porch*] We drive around the lake where all the rich folks live every Sunday afternoon with the sun on our faces and the wind in our hair.

MA HENRY: You better be driving around after church. I don't care where you live, the Lord always knows where you at.

VIOLA: Well, I don't mean to brag about my friends, but plenty of people have automobiles there. Not those old pick-ups, or sedans. But big fine cars. I've never seen so many Caddies! I can go out for a drive anytime I please.

CLYDE [*undoing his tie*]: Don't sound like that leave much time for workin' up that way, just a bunch of high livin'. What you getting into up there?

VIOLA: It's so nice of you to worry about how I'm gettin' along, Mr. James. Take a look at me though? [*Spinning around*] Do you see a reason to be concerned?

[CHERRY *returns from the kitchen and puts* MA HENRY*'s slice of cake on her lap, then turns to her cousin who is standing.*]

CHERRY: Here's your cake, Vi.

CLYDE [*taking his slice of cake*]: Ain't nobody studyin' you, woman.

MA HENRY: Clyde, she's doin' office work up north. Don't you worry none 'bout her.

CLYDE: Is that right?

CHERRY: Ain't no shame in doin' a honest day's work no matter what it is. As long as you right with God can't nobody else say a thing.

VIOLA: What's all this talk about shame and honesty? That's what I like 'bout Chicago. It ain't no sin to be proud and speak your mind. We don't need to be afraid all the time. Colored folks don't have to always clean houses for whites so they can eat. We can be anything we want in that city. It's an opportunity to utilize all talents.

CLYDE: With your talent being singin'? I guess you mostly utilize yourself at some kinda juke joint?

VIOLA: Hush now, Clyde. I do work, sugar—just like Ma Henry said, in an office downtown. But I've been waiting to tell y'all about my big surprise. Ole' Clyde's 'bout ta drag it out of me.

MA HENRY: Come on. Tell us your surprise!

VIOLA: Well, when I get back home I'll start as a featured singer at the El Grotto Supper Club. It's a big time blues club on the South Side of Chicago, Illinois!

CLYDE: Shucks, you tellin' us you practically a star?

VIOLA: Well now, I'm not tellin' y'all all that. But it is a great honor.

MA HENRY: Oh Lord! That ain't how we raised you to be singin' at no nightclub. Riding around in strange men's red Cadillacs. You need to quit that singin' job and find yourself a good husband.

CHERRY: What kinda songs you sing, Vi?

VIOLA [*annoyed*]: The blues kind, sugar.

CLYDE: My favorite kind of music!

VIOLA [*to* CLYDE]: Pretty ones, slow ones, fast ones, loud ones, quiet ones. [*Walking around* CLYDE *while he stands at rapt attention*] The blues tells stories that nobody forgets.

CLYDE: Seems to me I oughta go see you sing at this club in south Chicago.

CHERRY: I don't think that's on the way to California, Clyde.

CLYDE: When a man is travelin' alone it don't matter what road he takes.

VIOLA: Hmm. I'm confused. I thought you two were going together?

CLYDE: Is that right?

MA HENRY: Right or wrong she ain't goin' nowhere without a husband.

VIOLA [*staring at* CLYDE]: How about that! A husband for our sweet Cherry. Well Ma, maybe I'll go ahead and get married too someday. I might even sing me some lullabies.

[*Fade to black.*]

SCENE 4. SHADOWS IN MOONLIGHT

[*Evening.* CHERRY*'s bedroom.* CHERRY *is in bed reading* Lives of the Saints, *and* VIOLA *is sitting in front of the dresser, brushing her hair and singing softly.* MA HENRY *enters and watches them for a while from the doorway, then comes in.*]

MA HENRY: Cherry, don't be sitting up all night with that book of yours—you got a whole lot of work to do in the mornin'. Mrs. Fair expects you bright and early.

CHERRY: Yes, ma'am.

MA HENRY [*softly*]: Viola dear, that was real pretty today.

VIOLA: Thank you, Ma.

MA HENRY [*beginning to leave, but on second thought*]: You girls get some sleep. Don't forget you ain't too old to get on your knees to say your prayers.

CHERRY: Yes, ma'am. Good night.

VIOLA: Good night, Ma!

[MA HENRY *leaves the room.* VIOLA *says a short prayer, then starts to comb her hair again and hum to herself (a racy blues song) while* CHERRY *gets on her knees to perform an elaborate prayer. When she's done she lies down in bed, but tosses and turns. Each woman is aware of but ignores the other.*]

VIOLA [*pinning up her hair*]: You sleep yet, Cherry baby?

CHERRY: If I was, I sure ain't now.

VIOLA: What you and Clyde really planning on? What's on your mind, girl?

CHERRY: I don't need to tell you. Besides, you'd just laugh.

VIOLA: I won't! I promise on a stack of Bibles. You in love with him? You in love with old big-headed Clyde? Is that why you plan to run off?

CHERRY: I don't love no Clyde James. What do you care? Do you love him?

VIOLA: I don't think I ever been close enough ta real love to even smell it, let alone taste it. Anyway, what you know about loving? You ever *been* with a man?

CHERRY: That ain't Christian and you know it. Besides, you always running off to do what you want. Why can't I?

VIOLA [*sitting on* CHERRY*'s bed*]: We different, Cherry. Ever since me and you and Jefferson was little everybody said that. Remember your mama would say that Jeff and Vi cut from the same cloth, but that sweet ole' Cherry pie is a gift straight from God's own heart.

CHERRY: I don't remember nothin' like that! Vi, you tell tales worst than Clyde.

VIOLA [*laughing*]: And Clyde . . . tell me, sweet Cherry, have you kissed him?

CHERRY: What? I kiss my cross and Ma Henry. My lips ain't touched nothing else!

VIOLA [*goes back to the mirror to finish her hair*]: Is that right? I'm sorry to hear that. I ain't never heard of somebody kissin' their cross. Well, sugar, I'll be happy to leave this place so I can get my lips kissed again.

CHERRY: Vi! You hush now. You gonna need to pray again to cure all that sinnin' you thinking about doin'.

VIOLA: There ain't nothing sinful about a grown man and a grown woman doing what pleases them. Adam and Eve did it all day in the Garden before God's eyes! Doesn't your Bible tell you that?

CHERRY: I ain't readin' the Bible! I'm readin' the *Lives of the Saints*. I'm not listening to your bad talk! [*Loudly*] Now I lay me down to sleep. I pray the Virgin Mary my soul to keep, and if I dies before I see California I pray the Virgin my soul to take me to the beach.

[VIOLA *brushes her hair and sings Memphis Minnie's "Me and My Chauffeur Blues" to drown out* CHERRY*'s prayer.*]

VIOLA: "Won't you be my chauffeur / Won't you be my chauffeur / I wants him to drive me / I wants him to drive me downtown / Yes, he drives so easy, I can't turn him down." [*Laughing*] Girl! You so silly!

CHERRY: Don't you call me that!

VIOLA: What you fussin' 'bout ? Praying like that ain't gonna bring you nothing but sore knees. I know what I like and it's . . .

[VIOLA *lights up a cigarette.* CHERRY *jumps out of bed and walks over to* VIOLA.]

CHERRY: Vi! Put that thing out! Are you plumb crazy? I don't want to hear no more of your talk about men and lips and sinning! I'm not listening to that, Vi. You always talking about what you want and what you need but you never care about other folks. Don't you ever think about what Ma Henry needs?

VIOLA: You're the one leaving her for the wild west!

CHERRY: What about your own mama wiltin' away over in Shreveport? You see her a few days, come here and sing a little bit, and expect us to all be smiling when your train go? Maybe somebody else wanna go sometime. Maybe other folk got plans.

VIOLA: Plans, huh? Well I'll be. You do have a tongue in that head of yours. I don't think I've ever heard you talk that long in my entire life.

CHERRY [*climbing back into bed*]: I just ain't had much to say to you.

VIOLA: You soundin' like Ma Henry now.

CHERRY: While we at it, why didn't you come see us when Jefferson went away?

VIOLA: That's it right there. He didn't go away, Cherry. He was killed! He was hung out there in that land you call God's and choked on his own tongue.

CHERRY: Stop it!

VIOLA: No! No, I will not stop it. I'm gonna have my say.

CHERRY [*with measured anger*]: Viola Henry, you always have your say! I don't see why you always gotta talk like that? [*Holding herself and beginning to rock*] Why you haveta say those kinda things?

VIOLA: Don't you understand that I had to get out of this place? I needed to forget. Dusty roads and slow talking people. Women here cookin' all day or passing babies through their thighs. That's not how I want to live . . . spend my life slavin' in some kitchen for some white lady all day then come home to some drunk fool at night. Everything I got now is my own, Cherry. Night comes and if I want me some company? Not too hard to find somebody to sit with me. If I wants to make some lemonade with fresh strawberries and sit on my concrete stoop to watch the moon fly then that's how I'll spend my evening with no scratchy bearded man's supper to fetch.

CHERRY: Don't you care about us though? Don't you think about us? We are family, Vi. [*Pause*] I thought you was crazy 'bout Jefferson.

VIOLA [*after a pause*]: We use to swim out at Jupiter Pond all summer, remember? Shoot, even in winter we fell in a few times.

CHERRY: Then why didn't you come?

VIOLA: I just couldn't come back for his funeral. Y'all will have to forgive me, but I couldn't look at his face without being able to see the water shimmer in his eyes. Clyde the one cut Jefferson down from that tree, wasn't he?

CHERRY [*after a pause*]: Yeah.

VIOLA: So, you do love him?

CHERRY: No. Maybe. I don't know.

VIOLA: I appreciate all the love I get, even if other folk don't approve. [*Pause*] Can you take care of a man, Cherry? I know you can cook and clean, but honey can you take care of the haunting? A man who's seen something like that probably ain't no good for nobody.

CHERRY: What you mean, Vi?

VIOLA: I'm talkin' 'bout the haunting ghosts that come at night. Remember when we were girls—Ma Henry use to talk about how the ghosts of hung black boys float around after midnight? Not too many men can eat through that kinda pain.

CHERRY: You think they have ghosts way out in California?

VIOLA [*climbing into bed*]: Well, I do know there ain't as many up in the Windy City. But those places have their own style of haunting. [*Turns off the light*] And those ghosts from home follow you anywhere you go.

SCENE 5. LOOKING FOR JESUS

[*Later that same night. The only light on the porch is coming from the back rooms of* MA HENRY*'s house. Knock at the window and a distinctive whistle. It's* CLYDE *signaling for* CHERRY *to come outside.* CHERRY *walks out onto the back porch wearing her nightgown to look for the source of the whistling that woke her.* CLYDE *is standing in the shadows smelling a cigar; he lights it, and the glow from the match catches her attention. He's leaning against a car that* CHERRY *cannot recognize.* CLYDE *is still dressed in his Sunday best.*]

CHERRY: That you?

CLYDE: Who? You out here lookin' fo' Jesus, or you got yourself another boyfriend now?

CHERRY: Clyde?

CLYDE: None other. [*Waving his hands over his head*] Pack your bags! This here is our getaway car. [*Passing his hands over the vehicle*] We gonna—

CHERRY: Whose car is that, Clyde James?

CLYDE: Don't worry 'bout it. Come on and take a ride with me.

CHERRY: You sure you after me? Or you come here to show off for Viola? I betta call her so you can strut around here in the dark for her. [*With a fake cry*] Vi!

CLYDE: Oh hush.

CHERRY: That car stole?

CLYDE: Stole? Come on. Me? For a religious woman you sure worry plenty. Don't you know the meaning of trust?

CHERRY: I do. I trust deep in my heart that you done somethin' wrong this evening, Clyde James.

CLYDE: I'll prove it. I ain't guilty of nothin'! Come on down here to see the official ownership papers. Come on . . .

CHERRY [*walking tentatively down the steps*]: It sure is a fine automobile. [*As she gets closer*] Clyde! Oh sweet Mary! That's Mrs. Fair's Plymouth. Are you out of your mind?

CLYDE: Slide on in. You always said that woman got on your nerve right? Get in for a little minute. Let's go on over to Jupiter Pond and gaze on those stars. [*Tipping his hat*] The Milky Way is waiting, madame.

CHERRY: It's so dark out here. [*Standing at the car door*] How you expect us to see the Big Dipper tonight in this big old black sky? The moon is on the other side of the world.

CLYDE [*starting to sing and dance*]: "If you ever planned to motor west, travel my way, take the highway that's the best. Get your kicks on Route 66!" Come on, dance with me, girl!

CHERRY: Clyde, you are so crazy! They gonna send the police out after you. What about Mrs. Fair?

CLYDE: Is that what you need? A chaperone? Forget Mrs. Fair. Didn't you tell me about how that woman gets after tasting her sherry? I figure she's dead to the world 'bout now. Ain't nobody out here looking for that geezer or her car.

CHERRY: You've been drinkin' again, ain't you? You been . . .

CLYDE: I been thinkin' 'bout you. That's all that makes me smile. Been thinkin' 'bout asking you somethin' real serious.

[CLYDE *dances around and puffs on his cigar.*]

CHERRY [*waving the smoke out of her face and trying to get the car keys*]: Get from around here before Ma Henry come outside. Making all that noise. What's the matter with you?

VIOLA [*standing at the screen door*]: You found what you looking for?

CHERRY: I . . . Clyde—

VIOLA: Well, slap my face. Somebody out here looking like a real jive bomber!

CLYDE [*stopping his dance and tipping his hat*]: Evenin', Miss Viola. I bet you would take a ride with me in this fine motor scooter. [*Touching the hood*] Do your friends in Chicago get around like this?

VIOLA [*coming down the steps*]: Well, my, my, my. Is this yours?

CHERRY [*shooting a conspiratorial look at* CLYDE]: Viola, we better get inside before we wake—

VIOLA: Oh, Ma is out like a light. [*Advancing toward* CLYDE] Where we off to?

CLYDE: Anywhere you please, my dear lady. New York? Detroit? Even Los Angeles, California—you sure look like a star to me.

VIOLA: Let me go get my things—

CHERRY: No, you ain't getting nothin'. Clyde, you better take that car back over to . . . uh, Seymour's place. He's gonna be looking for it once he wakes up from his . . . spell. You need to go on and let us get some rest. Mrs. Fair expects me early tomorrow. Good night.

VIOLA: Oh Cherry, really. You oughta live a bit while you still free, beautiful, and young. Women like us have to grab life when we can. [*Touching* CLYDE*'s shoulder*] When a sweet man like this makes an offer—

[CHERRY, VIOLA, *and* CLYDE *notice an approaching car. They turn toward the audience and headlights show in their eyes.*]

VIOLA: Oh sweet Jesus . . .

CHERRY: Mary, Mother of God, full of grace.

[*As lights fade, the sounds of men yelling racial slurs and boisterous cries splinter the night.* CLYDE *runs off into the night as the voices call out for him to stop.*]

SCENE 6. WADIN' IN THE FLOOD

[*The next day.* CHERRY*'s bedroom at* MA HENRY*'s house.* CHERRY *is bedridden and weeping.* VIOLA *enters with a basin of water and a towel, stands for a moment watching* CHERRY, *then puts a cold compress on* CHERRY*'s forehead.*]

CHERRY: So much blood. Everywhere, the blood.

VIOLA: Try not to think about it.

[VIOLA *sits on the bed and holds* CHERRY*'s hand.*]

CHERRY: Just like Jefferson. The blood stuck to him like paint. That's how I remember my brother now. No smile, just blood. Like a painting of death.

VIOLA: Stop that talk!

CHERRY: Why can't I die? They always die for me. Why?

VIOLA: Rest. Ain't nobody dying today. Clyde knows this town better than anybody. He's gonna be fine, Cherry.

CHERRY: Jefferson knew this place too.

VIOLA: Clyde has better luck than Jeff, always did. Believe that if you believe nothin' else. [*Pause*] I didn't have a clue that he stole that car. I didn't think Clyde had it in him.

CHERRY [*Pause*]: Vi?

VIOLA: Yeah, sweetie?

CHERRY: I feel different. [*Beat*] The baby gone, ain't it?

VIOLA: Wasn't no baby, Cherry. That was all in your mind. The baby, Mary—that was all in your mind.

CHERRY: My mind?

VIOLA: A woman's mind is a mighty powerful thing. More powerful than her body sometimes. I think you just been too scared to let your flow come. Now, I guess you too scared not to.

CHERRY: Scared? They hung my only brother and I couldn't do a thing. Now Clyde—

[VIOLA *hugs* CHERRY. *They share a moment of silence.*]

VIOLA: Nothing we can do but wait to hear word. Your body needs rest, Cherry. I'll be in later to see about you. Get you some sleep.

[*Lights down.*]

SCENE 7. TRAVELIN' LIGHT

[*The sound of birds taking flight, then dogs barking and howling. Silence. Several days later. While* CHERRY *sleeps fitfully,* CLYDE *sneaks into the house. His face is cut, his clothes are wrinkled and bloody. He is badly bruised and one arm is bandaged. He stands over* CHERRY*'s bed and watches her sleep until she senses him and awakens.*]

CHERRY [*noticing* CLYDE]: Are you an angel?

CLYDE: I'm your angel. Yeah, it's me right before your eyes.

CHERRY: What you doin' here? You know everybody lookin' for you. This might be the next place they go.

CLYDE: Sure is, way I be talkin' 'bout your pretty smile all over town.

[CLYDE *starts to grab her but she pulls away.*]

Viola gone?

CHERRY: She's inside. You come back for her?

CLYDE: Don't talk like that. I never been sweet on Viola.

CHERRY: Where you been? Everybody is worried 'bout you. [*Pause*] I thought you was—

CLYDE: Dead? Naw! Those hooded fools can't kill a soul like me. I come back for you. I gotta know if you changed your mind 'bout coming to California with me?

CHERRY: What? Naw.

CLYDE: So, gonna stay in this place the rest of your life?

CHERRY: No. Yes—I don't know.

CLYDE: Then what you waitin' for?

CHERRY: I'm just scared is all.

CLYDE: Don't you worry, Cherry. Besides, I told you if you come on with me you ain't got a thing in this whole entire world to worry you.

CHERRY: Um hm—that's right, you did.

CLYDE: Surely, I told you I'ma take care of you.

CHERRY: I was tryin' to sleep but my dreams woke me up. [*Noticing a package in his hand*] Clyde? What's that?

CLYDE [*revealing a paper bag*]: I brung ya sumpin' special. Now let me at those toes.

[CLYDE *pulls the bedding away from her feet.*]

CHERRY: What? Clyde, don't be actin' all silly now. You already done stole enough. Somebody bound to come!

CLYDE: I ain't gonna hurt you. What's the matter? Why you still in bed?

CHERRY: I'm just restin' now. The worse is over.

CLYDE: The baby?

CHERRY: The baby was swept clean away. Viola said there never was one. I been so scared after they . . . they took Jefferson from me.

CLYDE: Me too. [*Beat*] You feelin' better? Your body all right?

CHERRY: I guess so. Truth is I wasn't ready to be nobody's mother, especially Jesus!

[CLYDE *hugs her, then looks into her eyes with recognition.*]

CLYDE: Trust me, Cherry. Just do as I'm askin'. You gonna be safe from all this if you go away with me.

CHERRY: So what's that you got?

CLYDE: Darlin', I got somethin' you sure gonna appreciate. Somethin' you need. Now relax yourself. Come on.

CHERRY: All right. I'm relaxin'.

CLYDE: Your feet are the most beautiful things I've seen in this ugly world.

CHERRY: Here you got the whole town chasin' you and you wants to see my feet? You know I ain't the type of girl that a man can treat any kinda way. That ain't how I was raised.

[CLYDE *grabs a pitcher from the nightstand and pours the water into a pan.*]

CLYDE: I know what kinda lady you is. A queen on this earth. The prettiest thing in Louisiana.

CHERRY: Clyde! You go on with that. What you doing?

CLYDE [*grabbing a towel*]: You been takin' care of everybody since you was a little thang. You cookin' for Mrs. Fair, nursin' on Ma Henry, and always got a table of pies for a True Vine Baptist social. You work so hard, Cherry. 'Low me to do somethin' for you.

[CLYDE *places the pan at her feet and takes a pink package out of the paper bag.*]

I found this at the store downtown with all those flowers and pretty trinkets.

CHERRY: That delicate place? Oh, Clyde.

[CLYDE *pours crystals into the pan.*]

What you doin'?

CLYDE [*kneeling and beginning to wash her feet*]: These is called beauty salts. I'ma treat you like the queen you is, Cherry. A queen, my queen.

CHERRY [*in awe*]: Ain't nobody in this world ever done me like this. Oh, that tickles. [*Laughing*] Well, this is mighty nice. I don't think anybody ever washed Mary's feet before. Nope.

CLYDE: I'm on my knees for you, Cherry. [*Taking her left hand in both of his*] I'm here to ask for your hand, official like.

CHERRY: Clyde, I . . .

CLYDE: Miss Cherry Henry, I'm here to ask you for your hand. I'm saying before God I gots to have you. I want to make you proud. Wants to make you my bride.

CHERRY: But, Clyde . . .

CLYDE: Hear me out now. I know we cain't see the future but I know I want that future to be with you. I've known you all my life and that don't have to end. I want to look on you when we both too old ta spit. Will you be my bride?

CHERRY: Oh my. No, I cain't, Clyde. I'm sorry . . .

CLYDE: Why not? What's the matter now? I always believed if I brung you out to California you'd marry me.

CHERRY: I don't think I can marry an earthly man.

CLYDE: I'll give up drinkin', smokin' if that's what you want . . .

CHERRY: It ain't that, Clyde.

CLYDE: What is it? I'm here in the flesh standing before you. I love you, Cherry, and I'm the one you oughta want.

CHERRY: Hush your sinnin' mouth, Clyde! Jesus is in my heart.

CLYDE: Girl, I'm tired of you. [*Beat*] Ain't we more to each other than that?

CHERRY [*beat*]: When those men came to get Jefferson I thought God would protect him, a preacher's son. I thought that God would bring him back to us safe. He didn't deserve that. You and I know that he was trying to protect me from harm. Me! He defended me from them boys and now . . . [*Pause*] He never came back, Clyde! He never came back breathin'. I remember when Ma Henry, Sister Thomas, and Natty and them laid him out in the house I could barely look at him. [*Begins crying*] You and I both know it wasn't enough of him to lay out. I stopped prayin' at True Vine after that.

CLYDE: You cain't run from everything, Cherry—you got to hold on to something right here on earth. Don't you know it can be me?

CHERRY: I don't know what to believe, I just know my loving never protect nobody from harm. I can't keep you from harm neither, Clyde. Maybe you oughta keep runnin' as far away from me as you can.
CLYDE: No! I'm ain't runnin' off alone!
CHERRY: Please, Clyde . . .
CLYDE: Let me keep you safe. Let me hold you. You let me kiss you and then you tell me that you don't feel nothin' for me. Let mc hold you, Miss Cherry, and tell me my love don't mean nothin' to you.

[CLYDE *takes her in his arms.*]

Lemme be somethin' to you. [*Hugging her*] Can I kiss you?

[CHERRY *nods, then* CLYDE *kisses her.*]

CHERRY: Mmm. Well, I ain't sure if one kiss can tell me all that.

[*Bashfully,* CHERRY *kisses him again.*]

I still ain't sure.

[*They kiss again.*]

This is a mighty big decision. What you think?

[CLYDE *kisses* CHERRY *deeply as the light fades to candlelight only. After a beat, the light comes up abruptly with* MA HENRY*'s entrance.*]

MA HENRY: Lord have mercy! Boy, what you doin' in my house?
CLYDE: Please, Ma Henry. Why don't you have a seat? I want to do this proper. I come to ask for Cherry's hand in the proper way.
MA HENRY: Clyde, you got the police and every Klansman from here to Texas looking for you! If you think you gonna take my precious grandbaby girl outta here so she can die by your side, fool, you got another thing comin'! I will not give you her hand or her foot or her ankle for that matter!
CHERRY: Ma!
MA HENRY: Hush girl! I'ma get to you.
CLYDE: I'm sorry, Ma Henry, but we leavin' with or without your blessin'—either way I know we got God's blessin'.
MA HENRY: What can you give her, Clyde? You ain't never been able to do for yourself!

CLYDE: A life, a new way to see this world. A woman need room and sunlight to grow just like those trees in that orchard.

MA HENRY: I won't have it, I'm tellin' you! If I had a switch I'd tear into yo' behind—both of ya!

CLYDE: I won't keep her here tied to graves.

MA HENRY: There ain't no more baby, you know?

CLYDE: Yes ma'am, I do.

CHERRY: He wants me for me. Not because of a baby. Me!

MA HENRY: Lord, have mercy! Girl, is this what you want?

CLYDE: Don't turn on her now, not when she needs you most. We want your blessing.

MA HENRY: This don't make no sense, running never solved anything.

CLYDE: Look across that creek at the graveyard and tell me what this place means. I'd rather die runnin' then stay here. I'd rather die with her at my side then alone like a dog in some ditch waitin' for a branch to hover over me. You can't keep her afraid of the world, the future, or her own body. I don't understand why you would even do that.

MA HENRY: Tell me why you think life would be any different way out there in California?

CLYDE: Willows don't grow on beaches.

MA HENRY: But there are other things that can kill a man. Viola's eyes look mighty dim, tell me, how I am supposed to believe in some place I ain't ever been and seen with my own eyes?

CLYDE: You ever been to heaven? Talked with an angel?

MA HENRY: No.

CLYDE: Ever walked on the clouds? You ain't never even seen God's face—but you believe, don't you?

MA HENRY: That's right.

CLYDE: It's called faith.

THE MAMALOGUES

DEVELOPMENT HISTORY

Colman Domingo directed Donnetta Lavinia Grays (Tasha), Roslyn Ruff (Beverly), and Sharon Washington (Lauren) in a reading of *The Mamalogues* at the HipHop Archive and Research Institute at Harvard University on March 7, 2011.

Shirley Jo Finney directed Cymone Love (Lauren), Carla Nickerson (Beverly), and Nadine Mozon (Tasha), in a reading of *The Mamalogues* as part of the John L. Warfield Center for African and African American Studies Performing Blackness Series at the University of Texas, Austin, on November 3, 2017.

PRODUCTION HISTORY

The Mamalogues had its world premiere at The Vortex in Austin, Texas, on August 23, 2019, produced by Color of Arc Productions (Christine Hoang, Artistic Director) in collaboration with The Vortex (Bonnie Cullum, Artistic Director). Stage management was by Cortney DeAngelo, dramaturgy by Virginia Grise, scenic design by Megan Kemp, lighting design by Patrick Anthony, sound design by Johann Mahler, photography by Steve Rogers. Rudy Ramirez directed the following cast:

Tasha Simmons .... Melody Fullylove
Lauren Holmes .... Yvonne Oaks
Beverly Franklin .... Valoneecia Tolbert

This script went to print on July 30, 2019, and does not reflect changes made during the preview period.

CHARACTERS

Tasha Simmons, a fifty-year-old African American mother. Widowed. Pediatrician. Soulful, sweet, and sassy. She's wearing a head wrap or has a natural hairstyle (afro, braids, or locks). She's wearing a colorful dress and comfortable sandals.

Lauren Holmes, a forty-nine-year-old African American mother. Single. College professor. Lesbian. Uptight, sarcastic, and tired. She has natural hair and wears minimal make-up. She is dressed in a crisp white dress shirt, a colorful and stylish cardigan, black pants, and loafers.

Beverly Franklin, a forty-one-year-old African American mother. Divorced. Salon owner. Calm, efficient, forthright and wise. She wears make-up and has straightened hair styled in a simple bob (perhaps with a tortoise-shell headband). She is dressed in a shirt, skirt, and stylish yet sensible low heels.

SETTING

Now. A cozy bed and breakfast or inn in a suburban town within a major metropolitan area in the United States. A retreat for a group for middle-class black single mothers.

PLAYWRIGHT'S NOTE

Although *The Mamalogues* centers the lives of middle-class black women, this play is a love letter to all black single mothers. It is a story also about family, sisterhood, and community among this frequently disparaged group. As the characters convey the disappointments, absurdity, and joys of single black motherhood, never allow the show to devolve into stereotype. The feel of the show should be intense yet playful as it presents each character's fertile imagination and vivid memories. Whenever possible, invite the audience to engage as if they are attending the retreat too. The rendering of each vignette should bounce between realism and the hyperreal as the women quickly morph into myriad other characters: family members, school administrators, and the random strangers who occupy their world. The set should have plenty of places to store props for the women to use as they assume different characters.

I also created a "mom-track" to help set the mood of the show. *The Mamalogues* playlist features soul, hip-hop, opera, and gospel songs about motherhood. The following playlist can be used for setting the mood at rehearsal, for the preshow, or as part of the sound design.

The Spinners, "Sadie"
Tupac Shakur, "Dear Mama"
Billie Holiday, "My Yiddishe Mama"

The Intruders, "I'll Always Love My Mama"
Lenny Kravitz, "Thinking of You"
Boyz 2 Men, "A Song for Mama"
LL Cool J, "Mama Said Knock You Out"
The Astronomical Kid, "Stop Looking at My Moms"
Kanye West, "Hey Mama"
Anthony Hamilton, "Mama Knew Love"
Gregory Porter, "Mother's Song"
Shirley Caesar, "No Charge"
Maxwell, "This Woman's Work"
Erykah Badu, "Ye Yo"
Jimmy Scott, "Sometimes I Feel Like a Motherless Child"
Loose Ends, "Be Thankful (Mama's Song)"
Gladys Knight & the Pips, "Hero (Wind beneath My Wings)"
Abbey Lincoln, "A Child Is Born"
Jaheim, "For Moms"
Dianne Reeves, "Better Days"
K-Ci & JoJo, "Momma's Song"
LL Cool J and Dru Hill, "Big Mama (Unconditional Love)"
Luciano Pavorotti, "Mamma"
Big Pun and Tony Sunshine, "Mamma"
Lauryn Hill, "Zion"
John Lennon, "Mother"
José James, "God Bless the Child"
Nina Simone, "Blues for Mama"
Earth, Wind & Fire, "Mom"

PROLOGUE. CLUB WOMEN

[*Lights up as* TASHA *enters from the house and mingles with the audience.* TASHA *is shortly joined by* LAUREN, *with whom she reluctantly shares the hosting duties. They have history. Both women casually greet and chat with audience members and engage with them as if they are also attending the retreat.* TASHA *and* LAUREN *eventually find seats. There is a buffet table laden with coffee, tea, and assorted finger foods and desserts in the room.*]

[*While* LAUREN *speaks,* TASHA *sits on a sofa and intermittently continues to quietly acknowledge women in the audience, especially any late arrivals.*]

LAUREN [*standing*]: Good afternoon! Good afternoon, ladies! I want to welcome you all to this year's BBSM retreat.

[BEVERLY *enters and finds a seat.* TASHA *waves to her enthusiastically.*]

Please enjoy the spread donated by Whole Foods and Trader Joe's. Before you ask, of course there are vegan and gluten-free options for our more discriminating eaters.

TASHA [*sitting on the sofa*]: And a slab of ribs for the rest of us!

LAUREN [*ignoring* TASHA]: It's good to see all of you! I'm thrilled to see so many new faces!

TASHA: Yes, look at all this melanin poppin'!

LAUREN: If this is your first time with us, I want to make sure everyone understands that BBSM stands for Black Bourgie Single Mothers—

TASHA: Not Bad Bitches Starting Mess—unfortunately, that name was voted down last year.

[TASHA *sucks her teeth.*]

LAUREN: And we don't want to see that posted on Facebook ever again, not even in jest!

[TASHA *rolls her eyes.*]

This group was established four years ago to provide a place just for us single black mothers—

TASHA: . . . of a certain age . . . [*winking*] and a certain income.

LAUREN: At Black Bourgie Single Mothers we come together to share parenting tips, recipes—

TASHA: Complaints about the dating scene in this tired-ass town, and good down-home gossip!

LAUREN: Tasha, please. Must you?

TASHA: What? Are you saying that we can't rant about exes being late with child support? We can't talk smack about people who send their kids to school with their hair wild?

LAUREN: That's not quite right, Tasha. I just think we must foster a positive environment where we celebrate our triumphs instead of always complaining about our challenges.

TASHA [*to audience*]: Well you can call me anytime so we can holler about *all* the drama. Girl, I got you!—

LAUREN: Moving along! [*Gathering herself*] Our group holds monthly gatherings to enrich ourselves by attending museum openings, book signings, film screenings—

TASHA: —and to keep us from being reported to Child Protective Services!

LAUREN: She's joking. You're joking, right?

[TASHA *nods unconvincingly.*]

I hope everyone is still feeling good after our spa visit last month.

TASHA: Hell yeah! I needed that.

LAUREN: Excellent! Remember, we're gearing up in a few months for our Shop and Bop. For those of you who don't know, it's a weekend excursion to Monterey for the Jazz Festival and to grab some deals at the premium outlet in Gilroy. I can't wait!

TASHA: Come on, Lauren, this group is not just about spa visits and positive affirmations. This is a space for support because Lord knows being a single mother is no joke—even if you are laced in Prada.

LAUREN: Of course we know that, Tasha.

[TASHA *takes a selfie with an audience member.*]

TASHA: We look cute!

LAUREN: Please take a moment to silence your phones so we can stay in the moment.

[TASHA *makes a big deal about complying.*]

Thank you! I know how hard that is for those of you who are attached to your devices, but let's be present. Since we have so many newcomers, let's take a moment to introduce ourselves. Tell us your name, about your kiddo, what you do for a living.

[*Awkward silence.*]

OK, I'll start! My name is Lauren, and I'm the current president of BBSM. I'm originally from Dallas, I'm an English professor, and I have a son named Phillip. Since you're in a talkative mood today, why don't you go next, Tasha?

TASHA: No problem, Ms. Lauren! Hi y'all! I'm Tasha. I'm the founder and former president of this little group. Now I'm the unofficial social secretary, AKA queen of the turn-up! I'm a pediatrician. My patients call me Dr. T. Yes, I'm the one who gives your kids all those shots they hate. I have a son and twin daughters. I call them my little jazz trio, but they're more like a rock band. Chile, those kids—

LAUREN: Thank you, Tasha! Why don't we hear from some of our other members?

[LAUREN *approaches a few women in the audience and ad libs with them, asking their name, occupation, how many children they have, and so forth. After speaking to one or two audience members, she points to* BEVERLY.]

Let's hear from you.

BEVERLY: Hi. I'm new to the group. My name is Beverly. I own a small business in town—

TASHA: Hey, Bev! Tell them about your beauty shop so you can drum up some more clients!

BEVERLY: It's a salon. We provide nail care, facials, hair care, and—

TASHA: Sis can do some hair too! Color! Weave! Cut! Even box braids. Tell 'em where it's at, chile.

BEVERLY: Thank you, Tasha. My shop is nearby. It's called Sweet Cuts. I'm originally from Houston. H-town, what's good? I have a daughter named Chelsea. She's six—going on sixteen!

TASHA: Girl! Tell it. These kids do the most!

LAUREN: Welcome, Beverly, and all—

TASHA: Anything else you want to add? Like how you heard about the group?

BEVERLY: Sure! Tasha suggested I come. She's my daughter's pediatrician.

TASHA: That's right! Give me my props. I'm building community up in here.

LAUREN [*trying to regain control*]: Yes! Yes, *we* are. Thank you for your contribution, Tasha. [*To the room*] Welcome to all of our new members. It's wonderful to see so many new faces! Ladies, the theme for today is sharing. Today's retreat gives us a chance for our members get to know each other better. In my classes I use icebreakers to facilitate conversation.

[TASHA *rolls her eyes.*]

I placed an assortment of questions in this little basket—

TASHA: That's so cute!

BEVERLY: That is!

LAUREN [*showing off a gorgeous rattan basket*]: Thanks! Home Goods!

TASHA: Girl! You know that store gets all of my check. All those knickknacks—

BEVERLY: They have nice bedding too.

TASHA: Girl! I can spend hours up in—

LAUREN [*motioning to the room*]: We should get back to . . .

TASHA: My bad! I'm sorry. Go ahead, Madame President.

LAUREN: I want to remind everyone that the theme for today is sharing. [*To the audience*] Valerie, stop rolling your eyes!

TASHA: You all game?

[LAUREN *looks at the audience for approval, while* BEVERLY *looks a bit uncomfortable.*]

LAUREN: Let's do it!

SCENE 1. BIRTH PAINS

LAUREN [*retrieving a slip from the basket*]: Aw! Here's a good one to start with. Tell us your birth story!

[LAUREN, BEVERLY, *and* TASHA *become a chorus of pregnant women engaged in a highly dramatic, loud, rhythmic Lamaze-style breathing. Very exaggerated.*]

ALL:

Ha ha ha ha
Ho ho ho ho
Hee hee hee hee
[*Pause*]
Ha ha ha ha
Ho ho ho ho
Hee hee hee hee
[*Pause*]
Ha ha ha ha
Ho ho ho ho
Hee hee hee hee

LAUREN: There is nothing more humbling than meeting new people whilr draped in a hospital gown and panting desperately every three minutes. We've seen it before, but somehow no movie, no TV show (or play) has ever represented that delicate dance. You know the one where a woman tries desperately to maintain her dignity—

BEVERLY: In a hospital gown.

TASHA [*as nurse*]: "I'm sorry darling, were you sleeping? I just need to draw some blood."

LAUREN: It was a teaching hospital and my doctor was a star on our local public radio station who spewed advice about women's health.

BEVERLY [*as male doctor*]: "There is rarely a reason to stop being sexually active. You can have sex during your final months of pregnancy, and well into your senior years."

LAUREN: I knew I'd made the right choice of physician.

TASHA: After your water breaks, make a mad dash to the hospital into the capable hands of the medical staff. There's nothing left to worry about.

LAUREN: Besides, you already made it through the godforsaken amniocentesis otherwise known as the—

ALL: "let it be healthy, let it be healthy, let it be healthy—"

LAUREN: But if it isn't—that's OK, I'll still love it—

ALL: "Thank God it's a healthy baby test."

TASHA: So, what's left to worry about?

BEVERLY: Right! I took all the classes. I packed my bag. I am officially ready to become a mother.

[*Trumpet blast.* TASHA *begins performing tasks as the lab tech.*]

LAUREN: After she sets up the monitors, I realize the technician is looking at me askance. Her forehead is wrinkled, her lips pushed out. What's the problem? Oh, she read my chart and now knows how old I am.

BEVERLY: My worries are temporarily interrupted by—

[BEVERLY *reacts to another contraction.*]

ALL:

Ha ha ha ha
Ho ho ho ho
Hee hee hee hee
[*Pause*]
Ha ha ha ha
Ho ho ho ho
Hee hee hee hee
[*Pause*]
Ha ha ha ha
Ho ho ho ho
Hee hee hee hee

BEVERLY: Pushing a baby out of my body is the hardest thing I've ever had to do. How do I summon the strength? My mind races to images from U.S. history. I see the slave quarters—no even worse, a slave ship—

[TASHA *and* LAUREN *hum mournfully.*]

I begin to imagine the unthinkable. Giving birth in the hull of a slave ship in sixteen nineteen. The unimaginable. The unspeakable. I begin to think of mothers in prison today. Right now. Pushing as I push, giving birth to babies while wearing leg shackles. And I push. I think of mothers giving birth to stillborn babies and I push and push and pray and curse and—

TASHA [*as doctor*]: "Push! We can see the head! It's crowning!"

ALL: Push! Push!

LAUREN [*as partner, friend, or family member*]: "Honey, push!"

TASHA [*as nurse*]: "Push!"

BEVERLY: And . . . [*heightened pause*] nothing. I push for over an hour but the baby won't come out.

LAUREN [*as baby*]: "Ah, no thanks, Mom. I'm good."

BEVERLY: There will be no crowning moment, no ultimate release. Instead? Instead there are drugs and cutting and—like thirty-three percent of American women in the twenty-first century—I received a single slash to my abdomen, now hidden in my bikini line. Thanks, doctor! Yes, a C-section.

LAUREN: C is not excellent,

BEVERLY: But it does represent a passing grade.

TASHA: Barely.

LAUREN: Yes, pushing out a baby is the single hardest thing that I have *never* done.

BEVERLY: The nurse holds her over the drape and we meet.

LAUREN: They clean him up and bring these eyes, this body, this voice over to me. It's our moment.

[*The lighting becomes ethereal.* TASHA *cradles an infant.*]

ALL: Baby cries,

LAUREN: And mommy cries,

TASHA: Partner/Friend/Nana/Nurse, somebody takes pictures—

BEVERLY: "Hey, get my good side!"

[*Theme song from* Roots *TV series plays.*]

LAUREN: I finally live up to my ancestral past.

TASHA [*mimicking the scene from* Roots, *she holds the baby over her head and up to God in ceremonial fashion, and, in an overly dramatic West African accent, says*]: "Behold! The only thing greater than yourself."

BEVERLY: I fulfill my womanly potential, I take my place among my sisters in the struggle, and I know.

ALL: I am a mother now.

TASHA: Now what?

BEVERLY: Do what comes natural?

TASHA [*as cheery nurse*]: "Welcome to Breastfeeding One-oh-One!"

LAUREN: The second most natural act in the world. I'm pumping milk while channel surfing. I land on a news story about people selling breast milk online.

TASHA: Wait! Is that heifer hawking breast-milk ice cream? Sweet Lord!

LAUREN: Yes! The modern day wet nurse has arrived. I can't imagine feeding somebody else's baby with my . . . boobs! My tatas! My breasts. My mind also turns to the slave quarters—

TASHA [*as slave woman*]: Missus slave owner ma'am, I just cain't suckle little Sandy Mae, Gilbert, and Overseer Jr. too—and you know, I think I have the mastitis. You know. That titty disease?

LAUREN: What is more unnatural than giving your breast to a complete stranger to suck? I can only imagine an infant tasting breast milk for the first time—

BEVERLY [*as a mature, annoyed baby*]: "No! Wait! This is not what was promised in the magazine ad. Besides, this breast is brown . . . logically, this should be chocolate milk and from what I can tell that is not chocolate milk. Wait? Is this soy? Rice Dream? Somebody tell me something, because the kid in the bassinet over there is actually very excited. So what's that Similac stuff? Can I get a hit of formula? Come on, I heard that the first suckle is free. Wait, let me dig in my diaper bag, I may have a coupon!"

LAUREN: Yes, there is something actually quite unnatural about motherhood.

SCENE 2. FORTY

LAUREN: Speaking of unnatural. How old were you when you had your first child?

TASHA: I have nothing to hide! My first baby popped out when I was thirty-four.

BEVERLY: I was thirty-five. How about you?

LAUREN: Well, I guess I win. I had my son at the ripe old age of forty.

TASHA: Yeah, she's a bad chick! The big four-oh!

LAUREN [*to the audience*]: Anyone got me beat?

TASHA: Look at us! A bunch of old mamas!

LAUREN: It's nearly a fad now, but remember just ten years ago? The whispers?

BEVERLY [*as a stranger*]: "Was it an accident?"

TASHA: "At that age?"

BEVERLY: "It's a miracle."

TASHA [*as grandmother*]: "Was you havin' one of them midnight life crises, sweetie?"

LAUREN: "How dare she at this age? It's just selfish!"

BEVERLY: "Absurd."

TASHA: "Dangerous."

LAUREN: People always want to know—

ALL: Why the hell did you wait so long?

BEVERLY: I mean . . . WHAT IF IT DOESN'T COME OUT . . . You know. [*Whispering—loudly*] *Normal?*

LAUREN: And the doctors!

BEVERLY [*as a doctor*]: "You must know that as a woman of advanced maternal age you will be involved in a geriatric pregnancy."

TASHA: My profession can be a bit shady!

LAUREN: That made me feel so scared.

BEVERLY: "Did you see her baby registry? Does she actually need all of this stuff? Can't she afford to buy her own stroller?"

LAUREN: Yes, I can! But I deserve this bounty after all my hard work. While that twenty-something couple got pregnant with a wink and a nod, I—like many other women with tufts of gray—spent many nights on my knees praying and countless hours in doctors' offices suffering through humiliating procedures just so that I can enjoy the miracle of life.

TASHA: I know that's right! I'll never forget the look of smug satisfaction on the faces of my family members. They never believed I'd slow down my career long enough to procreate.

LAUREN: Giving birth gained me entrance into that exclusive club, the sisterhood of motherhood. Yes, now I am truly an authentic black woman.

BEVERLY: Don't you know a bona fide black woman is a mama? You know, big mamas, mammies like the burly sister on the pancake box or the one screaming in *Gone with the Wind*!

TASHA [*imitating Butterfly McQueen as Prissy*]: "Miss Scarlet! Miss Scarlet!" [*As herself*] Yes! We are the mammies of the world! The bosom of civilization.

LAUREN: And once you have a child, those comments about having a baby are quickly replaced by—

BEVERLY: "So, when are you gonna have another? That poor, poor *only* child."

LAUREN: And my favorite—

TASHA: "I hope that that baby won't derail your career. After all—"

ALL: "You ain't no spring chicken!"

LAUREN: But it's not all drama. Sometimes motherhood at forty feels victorious. Miraculous. Yes, I'm also part of the "have-it-all" generation!

BEVERLY: Yay! We made it over the finish line before the race was called on account of faulty eggs. Look at me! I have it all. Lexus hybrid.

LAUREN: Check!

BEVERLY: House in the burbs—

TASHA: Check!

BEVERLY: Child with the cute name—

TASHA AND LAUREN: Check!

BEVERLY: Fabulous career that gives the false impression that the schedule is flexible—

ALL: Check! Check! Check!

LAUREN: But I'm doing this ALL alone. That's not having it all!

BEVERLY: Shush! Don't tell the other super-mom, Martha Stewartish size fours that I'm barely holding it together.

TASHA: Deal!

LAUREN: Now, if I cross paths with a woman whose baby hunger is palpable, I hold my child so close his eyes cross. That I am more blessed then anyone deserves becomes clear with each glance from the eyes of my sisters who pray for children, but whose miracle has yet to happen.

BEVERLY: And may never happen.

TASHA: So how do you explain to your child why you became a first-time mom at forty?

LAUREN: That's easy. I will answer without hesitation. I've been waiting for you all my life.

SCENE 3. WHO'S YO MAMA?

BEVERLY: That's really beautiful, but . . .

LAUREN: What is it?

BEVERLY: I have a confession to make.

TASHA: Girl, did you have booty call last night?

BEVERLY: No, Dr. Tasha. [*Under her breath*] I wish!

TASHA: Oh well. So, fess up!

BEVERLY: Sometimes . . . Ugh. This is going to be so hard.

LAUREN: Come on. Let's hear it!

BEVERLY: OK. Sometimes I wish I was not a mother. I wish I was just me. Nobody else to worry about. Nobody else to cook for. Clean up for. To be responsible for. God, I miss the days of staying in bed all day. Buying airplane tickets for one. Shopping for cute clothes only for me. Am I selfish? Am I too broken to be a mom? Alone? I wonder if I made a mistake.

LAUREN: I hear you. My life is divided cleanly. There was my life BB—before baby—and my life AB—after baby. I can barely recognize that these two lives were lived by the same woman. It's an extraordinary experience to go from navel gazing to . . . a different type of navel gazing.

TASHA: Tell it.

BEVERLY: Do I thank God for a healthy beautiful child? All the time, but . . .

LAUREN: Your kid is still young. It gets easier, Beverly.

TASHA: Don't lie to her. My oldest is sixteen and the twins are fourteen. Chile, it doesn't get any easier. Ever. It just gets differently hard.

LAUREN: I detect no lies. No matter how you're feeling—today, Beverly. We've got you. Right?

[*Motions to* TASHA *and the audience.*]

BEVERLY: OK. Here it goes. I hate Mama. I mean I hate the word "Mama."

TASHA: What? Now you done stepped in it!

BEVERLY: Not one matriarch in my family was ever called "Mama." I can't stand it. For me "Mama" evokes do-rags, lactation, and a very hot stove in a very small kitchen that she doesn't own!

TASHA: Watch it!

BEVERLY: Is that wrong? I just despise the sound of that word "Mama." I guess it's too close to "Mammy." I never once called my mother "Mama." My brothers and I always called our mother "Mommy." Not one of us *ever* called her "Mama."

LAUREN: As long as we are setting the record straight—to be honest, we never called my mother "Mama" either.

TASHA: You fancy Negroes are too much!

LAUREN: We actually called her "Mother." Plain and simple.

TASHA: That seems so formal. So . . . white.

LAUREN: I prefer proper. Classic.

TASHA [*under her breath*]: You would.

BEVERLY: Well, my grandmother was never called "Big Mama" either.

TASHA: Really? Too ghetto? Too close to "Mammy"?

BEVERLY: Maybe.

TASHA: Well, I always like "Moms." "Yo, how's your moms?" "Your moms sure can cook!"

LAUREN: Wait, Tasha, your kids don't call you "Moms" or "Mama."

TASHA: You're right. They just call me "Mom." Come to think of it, I've been black for five decades and I can't think of one black girlfriend who uses "Mama." Some of my white girlfriends do—I don't know what's going on with that exactly.

BEVERLY: One thing I do know is that I am and will forever be "Mommy." So when somebody asks—

TASHA: Do you love Mama?

BEVERLY: I guess we all have to confess—

ALL: We don't love Mama at all.

SCENE 4. HOMEWORK

[LAUREN *passes* BEVERLY *the cheese, then selects another question from the basket.*]

LAUREN: It may be the word "Mama" for you, but you know what sends me over the edge?

BEVERLY: What?

LAUREN: When people ask—

TASHA [*as a stranger*]: "Do you work outside the home?"

[*They all laugh.*]

LAUREN: Work? Outside the home? Outside? [*To audience*] Do we work, ladies? Raise your hand if you work! Not only do we work outside the home—

BEVERLY: We work on the side of the home,
TASHA: On top of the home,
BEVERLY: One hundred feet beneath the home!
TASHA: Damn it! We work—period!
LAUREN: And nobody is impressed, least of all other mothers! Professionals and mothers—
TASHA: Professional mother sounds kinda kinky—
BEVERLY: Well this kinky woman is exhausted!
LAUREN: We could all use some peace, quiet, a lavender-scented bubble bath, a slice of molten chocolate cake, and a glass of nineteen seventy-four Chateau Lafite Rothschild.
TASHA: You ain't never lied.
BEVERLY: But I'd feel guilty.
LAUREN: Right! How dare we feel joy?
TASHA: Be ambitious!
ALL: How dare we dream!
TASHA: After all we are living this life that's supposed to shame us?
LAUREN: Our name is on the tongue of every red-faced politician, and we're the subject of every study about the destruction of the black family.
BEVERLY: We're also the stars of every ghetto movie!
TASHA [*as stereotypical bad black mother, sucking her teeth*]: "Lissen, Terrell! I'm not up here to be played with!"
ALL: "You gonna learn today!"
LAUREN: How did we end up here?
BEVERLY: This was not the plan. He seemed like a great guy. He seemed like the one. He loved me more than anyone had ever loved me.
TASHA: They always do.
BEVERLY: But he did. Really did. I just didn't realize that I didn't love him enough to stay . . . forever. I needed passion. Romance . . . What did we get instead? Divorce. But not before I had a daughter. My precious girl. I wanted the whole package. Not weekend visitations and coparenting. Have I failed somehow?

[*The other women nod in sympathy.*]

What's your story?
TASHA: Well, I was happily married.

[*During this narration,* BEVERLY *appears as Ron. Solid, handsome, and full of life until the light suddenly goes out on him.*]

Ron was fine.

LAUREN: He was.

TASHA: He was younger than me, smart as a whip, and funny as hell. I had it all! An M.D., an M.R., and three big beautiful brown babies. Lawd, were we fertile! Did I mention he was fine?

LAUREN: You did.

TASHA: But he went to work and died at his desk. [*Pause*] Motherfucker!

BEVERLY: Oh my God. I never knew. I'm so sorry for your loss, Tasha.

TASHA: Thanks, girl. Me too.

[LAUREN *and* BEVERLY *hug* TASHA.]

LAUREN: My story is a bit different. My girlfriend Dana and I were on our way to having it all too. Then I realized that her "all" didn't include kids. So we broke up and I decided to stop waiting for Ms. Right before starting a family. I joined this sorority all on my own. I embraced single motherhood with a gracious donor.

BEVERLY: Good for you.

LAUREN: Well, I thought I knew what I was getting into. I read all the articles, the books, the studies. I entered into motherhood with my eyes wide open. Or at least I thought. But this life? This life right here is more than I bargained for.

TASHA: It doesn't matter how we got here . . .

LAUREN: Single.

TASHA: Widowed.

BEVERLY: Divorced.

TASHA: The world sees us the same.

ALL: Single. Black. Mother.

LAUREN: I can't help but think about my grandmother. How did she manage as a woman of great dignity but fewer means? A single mother who cleaned some other woman's house and watched *her* children and cooked *her* meals.

TASHA: And she did all of that so Betty Friedan could be liberated.

BEVERLY: As I hustle and complain I can't help but think of all the sacrifices my grandmother made, too.

LAUREN: When I was in college she sent care packages to keep me going as I prepared for a life so much better than she ever imagined.

TASHA: I think of my grandmother, mother, and aunts toiling through endless days and nights.

BEVERLY: How did they do it and retain not only their pride and sanity but a sense of grace?

TASHA: How did they manage all of that in the Jim Crow era, before the second wave of feminism and the invention of GPS?

LAUREN: How did you navigate those times? Can you send word from the great beyond? Heaven, can you send that angel back to me? I need some help finding my way. [*Beat*] I really miss my mother.

BEVERLY: I miss my mother too. Like a hunger. It hits hardest on holidays. Every Memorial Day I bake her triple-heart-attack butter pound cake to start the summer off right. Her voice is in every line of that recipe.

TASHA [*as* BEVERLY*'s mother*]: "Girl, buy the best butter you can afford. Don't skimp on the vanilla extract either. And make sure the batter looks just right before you pour it in the pan."

BEVERLY: The smell of that cake baking nearly takes me out.

LAUREN: Yeah, the holidays are hard, but I can prepare for those because they come like clockwork. But when I catch a scent on the breeze? The sorrow hits out of nowhere. Bam!

TASHA: Girl! Chanel No. 5 on the crook of her neck. Sunday mornings I always caught a whiff while she hurriedly buttoned my coat so we could make it to service on time. Chanel No. 5 makes me seven years old all over again.

LAUREN: For me it's witch hazel. Every night she wiped her freshly washed face with a cotton ball saturated with it. I've been using all these expensive concoctions for years, but the other day I decided to get back to basics. I stood at my bathroom sink, poured witch hazel onto a cotton ball, and had a visitation. The scent took me all the way back to the first time she wiped it on my pimply teenage face.

BEVERLY: The hardest part is knowing that my child will never know her laughter or know her stare!

[LAUREN *unleashes the certified "black Mama I'm not playing with you" stare. They all laugh.*]

My baby girl will never know how it feels to have her grandmother brush her hair and grease her scalp as she hums.

[BEVERLY *begins to hum a sweet blues tune. Other women feel this, nod and make sounds of deep agreement.*]

The moment when she touches your face and you know all is well with the world.

TASHA: Like a prayer.

ALL: Amen.

SCENE 5. LET THE CHURCH SAY

TASHA: Amen is right. [*To* LAUREN] Have you found a church yet?

BEVERLY [*as child*]: "Mom, do we believe in God?"

[*Sounds of pulsing, joyful gospel music. They are transported to church on Sunday morning.*]

LAUREN: Well, I guess I better find one soon. [*Stumped. Staring at the audience*] One of the most important jobs that you ever do for your child is to help them—

TASHA [*as a Baptist preacher*]: "Find a way out of no way."

LAUREN: At least that's what my grandmother said.

TASHA: Amen!

BEVERLY: These fast-paced modern times call on us to raise our children with a spiritual core.

TASHA [*as the preacher*]: "Praise Gawd!"

LAUREN: You need to find a place of worship that speaks to your soul.

[*Gospel music plays softly.*]

In the Baptist church you can find everything that you need to provide your child with a solid Christian foundation. I'm talking about history, redemption, and salvation.

TASHA [*as the preacher*]: "Beloved, this morning the choir will deliver the glory of Christ through song."

BEVERLY AND LAUREN [*chanting*]: Nam Myōhō Renge Kyō. Nam Myōhō Renge Kyō.

TASHA [*as the preacher*]: "What is that? Please turn your cell phones off!" [*Muttering*] "Ain't nobody trying to hear that noise in a house of worship. These chirren ain't got no sense!"

BEVERLY: Namaste.

TASHA [*as the preacher*]: "What did you say? Beyoncé?"

LAUREN: I hadn't been to church for years. I practice yoga and meditation, but I knew something was missing. Something that had shaped my young soul.

BEVERLY [*as Sunday black radio DJ*]: "Welcome to the Gospel Hour on WBLK where we play Mahalia Jackson, Edwin Hawkins, the Clark sisters, and the Reverend Shirley Caesar."

[*Classic gospel music begins to play softly.*]

The sweet sounds of glory. Thank you, black Jesus!

LAUREN [*reveling in the song*]: Those are the sounds of my childhood. I loved being in the choir at Good Shepherd Baptist Church. We sung all the songs I loved as a girl.

TASHA [*singing*]: Blessed assurance, Jesus is mine
O what a foretaste of glory divine
Heir of salvation, purchase of God
Born of His Spirit, washed in His blood . . .

ALL [*singing*]: This is my story, this is my song / Praising my Savior all the day long.

LAUREN: One Sunday morning the service took a left turn—

TASHA [*as the preacher*]: "I said that the Lord didn't create Adam and Steve. I believe the names were Adam and, much later, from his rib, the Lord brought forth his female companion, his helpmate, Eve."

LAUREN [*as the preacher*]: "Now you got these folks out here fornicating, sodomizing, and what not and then asking for the blessed sacrament of *marriage*? It's an abomination!"

BEVERLY [*as the preacher*]: "Black women can't find husbands because these so-called men are out here marrying each other. You better take that mess somewhere else!"

LAUREN: So I took my child somewhere else, praying that I'll find a righteous elixir to guide my spirit. I want a church with the soulful sounds of the Mighty Clouds of Joy—

[*A church organ punctuates every utterance.*]

ALL: Amen!

LAUREN: The communal pleasure of call and response—

ALL: Preach!

LAUREN: Church mothers dishing up soul food in the fellowship hall after the service—

ALL: Glory!

LAUREN: As well as a moment or two for quiet contemplation, meditation, and maybe some crystals—

TASHA: What? Have you done lost your cotton-picking mind!

LAUREN: Yes! You see, I just want to make sure that the call my child responds to—that my baby hears—is truly righteous, courageous, loving, and welcoming.

TASHA: "Black Woman! Black Woman! You wondering why you're alone? You don't know how to love a man and place him at the head of your household. You've got to *submit*! You'll never keep a man if you trying to wear the pants!"

LAUREN: Listen Rev, I like wearing pants sometimes and heading my own household.

TASHA [*as the preacher*]: "Don't follow those pro-choices folks. Out here slaughtering babies! Have them babies, Black Women, for when we are old and weary they will be the warriors that will protect our community."

LAUREN: OK, Rev, but who will protect us from you? [*Beat*] No, the search for a house of worship has not been easy.

TASHA [*as the preacher*]: "Then you got some women are out here having babies on they own like they can be the mother *and* the father."

LAUREN: I pray for a church home with soulful gospel music and gay couple support groups, yoga workshops, *and* fried chicken in the basement. I want a Sunday school where imaginative folk teach our sons and daughters the glory of prayer and faith. A space with a tutorial lab and a meditation room painted purple. Not only do I want my son to appreciate the choir's gospel sway, but I also want him to embrace the silent wisdom of Tibetan monks.

BEVERLY: The hustle these days means moving for career opportunities and leaving behind trusted pillars.

LAUREN: You hope your new life will grant you something almost as good—dare I say better? I don't see that on the horizon.
TASHA [*as the preacher*]: "Oh Lord, my Lord!"

[*Gospel organ begins to build to a crescendo.*]

"Congregation, are you there? Pick up! Pick up! Jesus is on the main line!"

SCENE 6. TRAVELING MERCIES

BEVERLY: Yes, you've got to pick up the phone and call on Jesus—

[*Sounds of a busy airport.*]

when I'm traveling with my kid. What about y'all?
LAUREN: Me too! There was traveling before motherhood—
BEVERLY [*laying the back of her hand over her forehead*]: "I'm so busy."
LAUREN: And there is travel after.
BEVERLY: Damn it! Where did I leave my—[*frisking her pockets looking for that elusive something*] child?!
LAUREN: We're easy to spot.
TASHA: There's one now! Moving fast!
LAUREN: Today's career woman arrives at the airport with her Tumi carry-on and rolling her eyes at the other people in line. Her prime adversaries? A family of four comprised of two parents, a brooding preteen, and a twisting, screeching toddler.
TASHA: Wait! Stop! Is that child . . . on a leash? It's not an animal, my God. If you can't leave the house without a bridle then maybe your family shouldn't be traveling.
LAUREN: Traveling while black and with a child is especially helpful on those "select your own seat" airlines. I love the fear I instill when they see us walking down the aisle.
BEVERLY: "Look! A single black woman with a baby!"

[*They all scream in horror.*]

LAUREN: It's not like I was very popular before I had a child, but now the blissfully empty seat beside us seems to be carcinogenic.
TASHA: "No, that's OK. I'll take that middle seat near the bathroom with that huge wad of bubble gum on the headrest."

LAUREN: Flying since the ripe old age of three months, actually my child is beautifully behaved—on most flights. I can't say the same for my fellow passengers.
BEVERLY: Did you hear about that white man who slapped that black baby on that Delta flight a few years back because he was crying?
LAUREN: Yes! That crazy fool slapped a black baby after he called him the N-word!
TASHA: Oh hell naw! I wish a muthafucka would try to slap my child! Y'all would have to put money on my books at the jailhouse for real.
LAUREN: You ain't never lied!
TASHA: Girl, I'd be locked up but that bastard would be six feet under!
BEVERLY: What kind of world is this? Now we gotta worry about somebody brutalizing our infants at thirty thousand feet.
TASHA: And we don't even get a meal on the damn flight!

SCENE 7. TERROR IN THE SUBURBS

TASHA: Traveling can be hell, but you know what else is scary?

[*Sounds of young children playing at the park.*]

LAUREN: Pools and parks!
BEVERLY: Agreed!
LAUREN: Here is my unofficial, very unscientific analysis, after visiting pools and playgrounds in Cambridge, Chicago, Austin, San Francisco, Portland, and Seattle. The farther west you travel, the more likely your little angel will be an OBC. [*To the audience*] You all know what that is!
ALL: Only black child!
TASHA: Wait, what about Oakland?
BEVERLY: Gentrified!
TASHA [*shocked*]: Oh mercy!
LAUREN: Here's how it usually goes.
BEVERLY [*as mother in the park observing* LAUREN]: "Lululemon duds, Birkenstocks, two-carat diamond studs, a stylish backpack—"
TASHA [*as another mother*]: "And organic snacks. Hmm."
BEVERLY AND TASHA: What's her story?
BEVERLY [*to* LAUREN]: "I haven't seen you before. So are you new around here?"

LAUREN [*to the other mother*]: Yes. [*To audience*] I've been spotted!

BEVERLY: "Wow! He's quite a swimmer."

LAUREN: Thanks.

BEVERLY: "How old is he?"

LAUREN: Six.

BEVERLY: "Wow! So, big guy! Are you going to be a football player? A basketball player?"

TASHA [*as child*]: "No, I'm going to be a physicist."

BEVERLY [*to child*]: "You don't say." [*To mother*] "Well, good for you!"

LAUREN: That's the stay-at-home moms. Wait until the nannies at the park get a bead on me. They try to locate my blond, blue-eyed charge; instead they spy my nappy-headed darling, and reality sets in.

TASHA AND BEVERLY [*as nannies*]: Ohhhhh!

LAUREN: Once the preliminaries are over, the playground small talk really begins. It starts out innocent enough.

BEVERLY [*as a mother in the park*]: "I heard a new Trader Joe's opened on Bee Caves Road!"

LAUREN: Inevitably, you find yourself hemmed up by the slides being queried about the aesthetic aims of Tyler Perry—

BEVERLY: The upcoming Cardi B concert.

TASHA: Okurrr!

LAUREN: The Obama presidency.

TASHA: "I wish he could do four more years! No, eight more!"

LAUREN: "Or my hair!"

BEVERLY: "Today you have braids. Last week you had an afro. How do you do it?"

LAUREN [*beat*]: But, once in a while you fall in love. Gazing across the grassy circle you catch each other's eyes and laugh at the same thing. You pocket your iPhone, she logs off Instagram, and the two of you actually talk.

BEVERLY: Mommy to mommy.

TASHA: Woman to woman.

LAUREN: And if you're lucky it actually becomes cherished chats and stolen moments on soccer fields, across Chuck E. Cheese tables, and whispers at the back of the library during story time.

BEVERLY: Friend to friend.

LAUREN: Once in a blue moon. Some wonderful miracle happens and you meet a mommy that gets you. No mommy wars. No competition. It's not fraught. It's not complicated. It's mother love.

[*Beat.*]

TASHA: Then it happens.

LAUREN: Something hits the news and she says something that pushes you off the integration tight rope.

BEVERLY: Your comments are carefully honed. Not too bitchy. Not too revealing. You share what you can and you hope she doesn't ask too much.

TASHA: You wonder if your visits on the playground entitle her to stories about your torrent of tears on that election night in 2008. Your nightmares about George Zimmerman. Your belief in reparations.

LAUREN: Are we girlfriends or are these moments simply an extension of her Bryn Mawr Anthropology 101 course? Is this really love, or just infatuation?

ALL [*in unison*]: I thought you were different.

LAUREN: After the calls stop, and the stolen moments end, we still have to maintain a relationship because of the children. You can't just break up . . . the friendship. So you find a way to make it work even though it doesn't work anymore. You see each other at the birthday parties and you suffer through prearranged play dates. It's back to small talk about shopping and the refs at the latest softball match. [*Beat*] But all that awkwardness evaporates when there is a tussle, cry, scream, or scrape.

TASHA: Battle stations, everyone!

BEVERLY: Every mom has a moment when she cannot find her little one in the running, screaming, frolicking mass of baby fat and snotty noses. The heart stops! Ice runs through her veins like *bad smack* (not that I know, but it sounds really cool).

TASHA [*cupping her hand to cover a Secret Service agent–style earpiece*]: This is a code red! I cannot get a visual! The threat alert is elevated. I repeat, the threat alert is elevated.

LAUREN: How can your heart stop and race at the same time? It's excruciating agony. It's the longest twenty-three seconds of your entire life.

BEVERLY: You scan the playground like a hawk. Your body swivels back and forth with utmost speed—those yoga and Pilates sessions were not in vain. You climb on a park bench and stand on your tippy toes to gain the best possible vantage point.

TASHA [*hand covering earpiece*]: Wait! There he is. I have the target. We have a visual. Fourteen yards due southeast. He's near the swings and sandbox. Stand down. He's all right.

ALL: Thank God!

LAUREN: No crazy-ass somebody traipsed off with my little prince.

[*They participate in a collective and audible heavy sigh.*]

TASHA: But what if he was missing? I find it hard to imagine a news anchor wringing her hands as she testifies to the purity and innocence of a missing little black boy.

BEVERLY [*Nancy Grace–style*]: We are missing a Negro—I'm sorry—a black African American child, male. Is that right, Kirsten? Yes, it's a small African of American heritage who was *allegedly* playing in the park. [*Examining her notes*] Hmm. That's a good neighborhood too. You usually don't find those kind of people, I mean that kind of thing happening there.

LAUREN: When was the last time the authorities released an Amber alert for a missing black boy? What do they even call it?

TASHA: A Tyrone alert?

LAUREN: A Rasheed response?

BEVERLY: An Antoine alarm?

LAUREN: No, there is no alert for abducted black boys.

TASHA: But everybody is on the lookout for them—to cause trouble. If a black boy talks too loud . . .

BEVERLY: Moves too fast . . .

LAUREN: Or acts too energetic . . .

TASHA: There is no timeout or warning. Instead?

ALL: There will be consequences.

BEVERLY: If there is no "school safety officer" to subdue him the child will promptly be sent to the principal's office. There he'll receive a suspension, a referral for some ADD meds topped off with a call to a behavioral therapist—

TASHA: Or, worse—

ALL: The police.

TASHA: This completes our tour of the school to prison pipeline. Have a nice day!

[*They all wave cheerily.*]

BEVERLY: Yes, we are parenting while black and living in the age of anxiety.

TASHA: Wait! "The age of anxiety"? Really? That's such a grand self-indulgent phrase. It's spoken like this is some kind of a unique moment in American culture. Black parents were a bit anxious when the Klan was outside the door.

BEVERLY: And we can't forget about the era of school desegregation?

TASHA: What desegregation?

LAUREN: How dare I complain? My child attends the best suburban school within a two-hundred-mile radius. My biggest concern is whether he receives fair treatment at the science fair. [*Beat*] Nothing to fear here.

TASHA: No Amber alert. According to news reports, nobody is taking innocent little black boys and girls off America's streets. But they are dying anyway.

BEVERLY: Chicago?

LAUREN: Can we save them?

TASHA: Oakland?

LAUREN: Will we save them?

BEVERLY: New York?

LAUREN: Anyone trying to save them?

ALL: Memphis? Cleveland? Philadelphia? Detroit? Atlanta? New Orleans? St. Louis? Houston? Baltimore? America?

BEVERLY: Do you want to save them? Any of them?

TASHA: Can we get an Amber alert for Tanisha and Tyrone?

LAUREN: Everyone cried for Polly Klaas, Caylee Anthony, Natalee Holloway, and Amber Hagerman, but nobody cries for brown babies.

BEVERLY: How could we, when missing black girls never make the news?

ALL: Say her name!

TASHA: And little black boys? Well, we know their fate.

LAUREN: Our friendships will always have unfilled silences because they don't know what it feels like to be missing and never sought after.

ALL [*furiously waving good-bye*]: See you at the park!

SCENE 8. THE N-WORD

TASHA: What's the worst moment that you ever experienced as a mother?

BEVERLY [*as child*]: "Mommy! Mommy! What's a nigger?"

LAUREN: Ah. The four-hundred-year-old question. So, how did Mommy answer that one?

BEVERLY: I remember when I first heard it. I was in kindergarten. I was wearing my pink polka dot dress and a white satin bow and a buttercream ivory slip—a slip, remember those? White stockings and squeaky snow-white patent leather shoes. My four ponytails braided and bangs, banging. I mean the do was tight! I was pressed and curled and ready to shine! OK, I don't really remember all of that. I only recall it with such stunning detail because it was picture day. Yes, I have a photo to commemorate the day somebody first called me—

ALL [*as school bully*]: "Nigger."

BEVERLY: The word was spat at me by the girl all the kids called—

ALL: Dirty Mary!

TASHA [*as Dirty Mary*]: "My Mama said your skin is black because NIGGERS. Don't. Wash."

BEVERLY: I was completely appalled and especially mortified because *she* said it to me. Mary was a portly, unkempt, blond and ruddy bully. What she lacked in style she made up for in meanness. Mary's family rented that house on the corner with the peeling yellow paint and patch of dirt where the grass should grow. It was rumored that Mary had poor hygiene. I don't know because I never got close enough to her to find out. So I was shocked when Mary said—

TASHA: "Your skin is black because NIGGERS. Don't. Wash."

BEVERLY: Black people don't wash? We don't wash? That's strange because I remember being soaped, soaked, and scrubbed until a rash developed. Then I was slathered with lotion.

LAUREN: Jergens!

BEVERLY: And oiled—

LAUREN: With Vaseline.

BEVERLY: Until I slipped effortlessly into my clean undies. I was brushed and combed each morning and night until I sparkled. Excuse me. Did you see what I am wearing? How can *she* disparage me?

TASHA: So what did y'all tell your kids about THAT word?

LAUREN: Not yet. He's too young, besides I don't use it myself.

TASHA: Really?

LAUREN: No, do you?

TASHA: Well, there's the N-word and the friend word. You know, "nigga." You gotta teach them the complex difference between the two. The despicable term and term of endearment. My kids know the difference.

BEVERLY: You can do as you wish, but I couldn't discuss *that* word with my baby girl. I told her not to worry about it. I don't want to cripple my child with the horrors of American history and the twenty-four-hour news cycle littered with black bodies.

LAUREN: It's just too much.

TASHA: Well, we can't stay silent. Are you going to wait until somebody like Dirty Mary does the honors? It's hard, but folks must find ways to talk with their black, brown, yellow, and white children about race.

BEVERLY: Not yet. Not yet.

TASHA: What if a stranger approaches your daughter on the street and wants to give her candy?

BEVERLY: I already told her if that happens that she should run like hell!

TASHA: Did you tell her to run outside if the building catches on fire?

BEVERLY: Of course!

TASHA: What's the difference? No child should face that word without the proper training.

LAUREN: Well, I'm going to give my baby boy the best offense and defense. I'll shower him with all the "you are black and beautifuls" that his little ears can hold.

TASHA [*as child*]: "Mommy, what should I say if somebody calls me a nigger?"

BEVERLY: Tell them—

ALL: Your Mama!

SCENE 9: CAMP

TASHA: Somebody better pray for this mama because summer is coming and I've got three kids at home. Jesus!

BEVERLY: Call on the Lord and He will deliver the answer.

BEVERLY [*as Camp Race R Us spokesperson*]: "Tired of sending your brown little jewel to integrate yet another camp? Are you struggling to raise healthy, balanced, smart, happy, and nappy American children?"

ALL: "Welcome to Camp Race R Us!"

TASHA: "We realize what it takes to raise a black child in America. You can't allow them to have fun, play videogames, or plop them in front of the television *ever*! Daydream? Have you lost your mind?"

BEVERLY: "Maybe! The high school dropout rate for black boys is at epic proportions, and black girls are punished in school more harshly than any other group. In this world of preschool entrance exams, helmets, knee pads, and Latin tutors, you can't allow your black child to experience the summer slide."

LAUREN: "But don't you worry! We will help your little brown brainiac slaughter the SAT and the ACT, but we provide more than academic enrichment. You see, I started this company because strangers kept approaching me at Whole Foods asking for help. How do you do it? Your child seems so smart, well balanced, happy, and so . . . black. I mean just the right amount of black."

TASHA: Yes, it's essential to teach your black child how to be black. This doesn't come naturally you know, especially if you're raising your black baby in the burbs.

LAUREN: By the time they enter school they must be well versed in the dynamic of racial victimhood. They need to know how to—

ALL [said in *Wheel of Fortune style*]: Play! The! Race! Card!

TASHA: Not picked for dodge ball?

ALL: Racism!

BEVERLY: Always *It* during tag?

ALL: Racism!

LAUREN: Nobody will sit with you during lunchtime?

ALL: Racism!

TASHA: No teachers or administrators of color at the school?

ALL: Ra—

BEVERLY: Hey y'all, all of that could actually be racism.

LAUREN: You're right.

[*They all nod furiously.*]

BEVERLY: "When your child grows a bit older and reaches the preteen years, Camp Race R Us provides a special session for those who lack firsthand experience with persistent racial violence. Our most popular session?"

ALL: Police harassment.

BEVERLY: "At this exclusive session, young boys are given elite training on how to lie face down on the pavement, put their hands behind their necks, and say—"

LAUREN: "Yes, sir!"

BEVERLY: "Loud enough to be heard even when a peace officer has a knee in his back. Your sons will also learn to NEVER reach for anything in his pocket—EVER. Repeat after me, young black men—"

ALL: "NEVER reach for anything in your pocket EVER!"

BEVERLY: "Because it just may be the last thing you ever do." [*Beat*] Rest in peace.

ALL: Amadou.

BEVERLY: Rest in peace.

ALL: Trayvon.

BEVERLY: Rest in peace.

ALL: Sean.

BEVERLY: Rest in peace.

ALL: Oscar.

BEVERLY: Rest in peace.

ALL: Michael, Eric, Freddie, Walter, Philando, Tamir.

[*Pause.*]

BEVERLY: "Don't worry, your daughters won't be left out at Camp Race R Us. Your daughter will emerge able to navigate the intersection of racism and sexism and be able to detect whether she's facing discrimination because she's black or a woman—"

TASHA: Or both.

[LAUREN *and* TASHA *demonstrate each behavior as* BEVERLY *describes them.*]

BEVERLY: "If girls opt for the Sandra Bland track, they will learn how to resist the urge to engage in the following behaviors: finger pointing, hand on hip, neck rolling, teeth sucking, and eye cutting when encountering a white person working in an official capacity."

TASHA: This is important knowledge.

LAUREN: "Girls will also make quilts adorned with the names of our fallen sisters, daughters, mothers, and grandmothers."

ALL: Rekia Boyd, Korryn Gaines, Charleena Chavon Lyles, Aiyana Jones, Eleanor Bumpers.

[TASHA *thrusts her fist high, and the others join her.*]

TASHA: Rest in power.

BEVERLY: "Wait, there's more. At Camp Race R Us, we can show your little one how to avoid being picked on by their [*fist pump*] 'I am blacker than you' cousins. [*Super corny*] Yes, an afternoon session can teach your little one to twist up a joint like Snoop Dog. Wait, a little too real? Don't worry, it's not really weed, only parsley."

TASHA: "As for classroom exercises? There are plenty! Topics include:"

LAUREN: "How to spot a teacher who expects very little from you because of your high melanin count."

BEVERLY: "They will learn how to tell 'Your Mama' jokes, cornrow, and make red beans and rice."

LAUREN: Yum!

TASHA: "Finally, they will be taught how to challenge the librarian about the lack of books featuring black people. Sorry, Negro History Month selections do not count."

LAUREN: "There is no reason for your darling to navigate the changing racial climate on their lonesome. Our devoted culturally competent counselors will answer all of their troubling little questions about what it means to be black in the #BlackLivesMatter era."

BEVERLY: "Yes, at Camp Race R Us your little BAP—bourgie American prince or Black American princess—will become a militant/athlete/culturally aware thug, and maintain a four-point-three GPA, all while nurturing their artistic side."

LAUREN: "Send your baby to Camp Race R Us this summer."

TASHA: "Enroll now!"

BEVERLY: "Spots are going fast."

LAUREN: "They are guaranteed to leave ready to play a card—"

ALL: "Any race card!"

[*Hip-hop beat begins to play.*]

SCENE 10. SO FRESH AND SO CLEAN

TASHA: Whew! I've been triggered.

BEVERLY: Me too!

TASHA: I'm craving something . . . sweet.

[TASHA *sorts through the food on the table.*]

BEVERLY [*slathering Brie on a cracker and holding it up for all to see*]: Yes, but I prefer savory. I can't live without good cheese. That calms my nerves.

LAUREN: Yes, comfort food always takes the edge off. I just don't know what I want.

TASHA [*finding a box of chocolates*]: There it is! A big hunk of dark, thick . . . chocolate.

[*Everybody laughs. To* LAUREN *mockingly*]

I know what really calms you down, Miss Lauren.

LAUREN: Don't you dare!

TASHA [*as* LAUREN*'s housekeeper*]: "Do you need anything else, Miss Lauren?"

LAUREN: No. That's it, Susie. Thank you so much for everything.

TASHA: "Yes, of course, Miss Lauren."

LAUREN: I don't know how I'd be able to manage without your help. You save my life every week! I do have one favor to ask. Susie, can you please stop calling me "Miss"? Lauren. Just Lauren.

TASHA: "OK, Miss. I mean . . . Lauren."

LAUREN: How is your son doing in school?

TASHA: "I miss him so much. Every day. He calls me from the college and he say, 'Mama! Send me roti. Mama, I can't find any clean clothes. Mama, did you pay my cell phone so I can use it?' "

LAUREN: I can't believe he's in college. Wow. You must be so proud! Those kids! [*Handing her an envelope.*] Thank you again for everything.

TASHA: "Thank you so much, Miss." [*Noting the additional money*] "You are so kind for me. Too good."

LAUREN: You deserve every bit. Those college textbooks are so expensive these days!

TASHA: "Yes. You are very kind. See you next week, Lauren!"

[*Beat.*]

LAUREN [*to her friends*]: She's my rock. A few days after Susie's cleaned it's back to being a hot mess. But when she first leaves I look around and don't want to touch a thing. I just sit in my living room and admire her handiwork and breathe. [*Beat*] Am I less of a woman because I allow another to clean my stove, wipe down my countertops, mop my floor, empty my trash, and [*whispering*] scour my toilets?

TASHA: Maybe.

LAUREN: It took me decades to discover that my grandmother, my regal grandmother, did the same work—day work they called it back then—to keep my mother and her four little brothers fed. She hid it from us. She and my aunts told us they were nurses. Grandma used to tell me stories about the family she worked for. Somehow it never occurred to me that nobody hired nurses with a junior high school education.

BEVERLY [*as Grandma*]: "Those folks relied on me to keep that big old house from going to the dogs. They needed me to keep 'em alive! Without women like me this entire country would fall apart!"

LAUREN: I often wonder what Susie really thinks about me.

TASHA [*as she finishes cleaning and packing up hand-me-downs*]: "She thinks I want her old clothes and used furniture. I work for what I have. I don't beg. I don't ask. I don't need hand-me-downs! I don't have a husband either. We aren't any different in that regard. A little extra? I deserve every cent and more. She's not as bad as the rest, but sometimes I can smell her guilt as soon as she opens the door. It stinks. I want to tell her: you don't need to feel ashamed. Relax. Sister, I'm proud of the work I do. I wish you were proud of it too. But that's not my job."

SCENE 11. MUCH IS EXPECTED

BEVERLY [*to* LAUREN]: Can I ask you something?

LAUREN: Sure.

BEVERLY: What's really important to you besides being a mother?

LAUREN: My writing. It keeps me sane and allows me to make order of the world. If I had to say, it would be that.

BEVERLY [*to* TASHA]: And you?

TASHA: My community. Giving back is essential. It feeds my soul. What's that saying? [*Placing her hand to her ear to encourage audience participation*] "To whom much is given . . ."

ALL: "Much is expected."

TASHA: Yes, that's right! Y'all got some good home training. Go ahead! Let me ask you something. If I am my ancestors' wildest dreams then why am I still dealing with their worst nightmares? *Some* people are surprised when I tell them that I'm a doctor.

LAUREN [*as a stranger*]: "Do you practice on people?"

TASHA: No, I practice on dolls until I can work myself up to taking care of humans.

LAUREN: "Oh."

TASHA: But when I tell *my* people I'm a doctor they respond differently.

BEVERLY [*as* TASHA*'s patient, Yonnie*]: "Yes, she's a doctor. A goodass doctor too."

TASHA: I've been in a private practice for twenty years, but I also volunteer on a health mobile where we give general medical attention to those who can't afford it.

BEVERLY: "What's up, Dr. Teeeee!"

TASHA: She was my favorite on again, off again patient. Let's just call her—

BEVERLY [*as a loud, exuberant, bodacious, and lovely patient*]: "Yonnie. But you can call me, Yon! You know, like you're tired."

TASHA: After a long day of seeing patients, she made me feel like I was sixteen again and wild. [*To* BEVERLY] You didn't finish the forms, Yonnie.

BEVERLY: "I ain't trying to do all that, Doc. Come on. You just ask me shit and I'll tell you shit. Is that cool?"

TASHA: You still working at the Pancake House?

BEVERLY: "Pancake House? Naw, Doc. I stopped working there months ago. I'm doing online training to be a dental hygienist. I'm gonna be wearing a little white coat like you soon!"

TASHA: Yonnie, what was the first day of your last menstrual period?

BEVERLY: "Damn, can you buy me a drink first before you're all up in my business?"

TASHA: You know how this goes.

BEVERLY: "A few weeks ago? Maybe."

TASHA: OK. Hmm. Do you have breast tenderness? Are you experiencing fatigue?

BEVERLY: "Uh huh. I'm tired all the damn time but that ain't nothing new."

TASHA: So, we should do a test.

BEVERLY: "Fine." [*Beat*] "How much school did you do to become a doctor? It must have been like, forever."

TASHA: Almost.

BEVERLY: "You happy looking at women's private parts all day?"

TASHA: It's an honor to take care of women and help them take care of themselves.

BEVERLY: "I heard that. Folks gotta call you doctor too so that's dope."

TASHA [*to* BEVERLY]: You're thirteen weeks pregnant.

BEVERLY: "Really? Lucky thirteen. And that means—"

TASHA: It means you will have another beautiful baby in six months.

BEVERLY: "And?"

TASHA: It's too late to terminate.

BEVERLY: "Terminate?"

TASHA: I can also share information about adoption.

BEVERLY: "Give my baby up? Naw, I'm good, Doc. Keep that information. Tell me where I can find me a job with some health insurance and some maternity leave. I hope it's a baby girl. I've always wanted a girl. I could braid her hair, teach her how to double-dutch and play jacks. What? Don't look at me that way. I've got this. It's all good!"

TASHA: I invited her to my private practice. The staff twisted their lips up some but nobody said anything. She came when she could.

BEVERLY: "I'm doing the best I can! Damn! If I don't show up to work, I don't get no check. I can't feed my children on medical appointments. I'm doing good. I eat, I sleep when I can, I take those huge-ass pills."

TASHA: Prenatal vitamins.

BEVERLY: "Whatever. They give me gas."

TASHA: And drink plenty of water. No soda.

[BEVERLY *sighs.*]

You've got to stay off your feet as much as possible. Please, Yonnie. I don't like what I'm seeing here. Your numbers are too high.

BEVERLY: "Doctors always say that shit. I'll be fine. Besides, what am I supposed to do? Stay off my feet? Please. This ain't no fairy tale.

Nobody is keeping me in a big castle so I can stay at home all day and put my manicured feet up. Even on my days off when Mike don't come get the kids. Bed rest? I can't even get couch rest. My pops retired last year but he still picks up a few shifts doing greeting at Walmart. He comes when he can to play with the boys. Bless him. He's all I got."

TASHA: A few days before her due date she was admitted to the hospital. Her blood pressure was obscenely high.

BEVERLY: "Preeclampsia? What's that?"

TASHA: When the attending called me I rushed to the hospital to see about her. I was reviewing Yonnie's chart when the team came out of the O.R.

LAUREN [*as other doctor.*]: "I'm sorry. We did what we could. We did what we could."

[*Beat.*]

TASHA: Yonnie had a baby girl. Her first. One of her aunts eventually named her Grace. That day I finally met Yonnie's sons. Her eldest, Joshua, was holding an old Game Boy; her youngest boy, John, gripped a green race car.

LAUREN [*as John*]: "Ma'am, are you the doctor?"

TASHA: This is one of the times I want to say no. [*To the child*] Yes, dear. I'm one of the doctors here.

LAUREN: "Wow, I never met a black woman doctor. Doctor, is my mommy OK? I'm an older brother now. Is the baby big? Is it a boy or a girl? Can I see them? Please? Can I see them?"

TASHA: I was devastated. Black mothers are dying every day.

[BEVERLY *takes* TASHA*'s hand.*]

LAUREN: That could have been me.

BEVERLY: She could have been me.

TASHA: It could have been—

[LAUREN *takes* TASHA*'s hand.*]

ALL: Me.

[*The women embrace* TASHA *as she cries. The circle of sisterhood is tight.*]

SCENE 12. SOCCER MOM

TASHA: I'm gonna need something stronger than chocolate to get me through this. What else we got?
LAUREN: Ask and she will provide.

[LAUREN *pulls a bottle of wine out of her purse.*]

BEVERLY: Nice!
TASHA: Wine? That's all you got?

[LAUREN *flashes her a look.*]

OK, OK. I'll take it.

[LAUREN *pours everyone a glass of wine.*]

LAUREN: I think we all need a bit of something. You know I don't mess with anything stronger since you got me drunk freshman year. [*To the audience*] Who else found out about that dark liquor in college? Show of hands!
TASHA: Guilty as charged. Hasn't stopped me from getting my drank on once in a while.
BEVERLY: Wait! You know each other from college?
TASHA: Yep.
LAUREN: Roommates. Learned a lot about each other in that dorm room.
TASHA: Close quarters makes for close friends or lasting enemies.
LAUREN: Or a little bit of both.

[TASHA *and* LAUREN *both laugh.*]

BEVERLY: I'm curious. What did becoming a mother teach you about yourself?
TASHA [*as white parent at school*]: "Incredible! He really plays so well. He's simply a natural!"
BEVERLY [*as another white mother*]: "Please let him join the soccer team! All the kids head over to the field after school. Molly organizes the carpool and I'm sure she could run him over to the—"
LAUREN [*to the other mom*]: No. I don't want him on *that* soccer team. He actually belongs to a team on the east side. In the hood.
TASHA: "I see."

LAUREN: I'd seen enough. I had my fill after witnessing the Tyler twins scream at their mother to—

BEVERLY AND TASHA [*as bratty tween twins*]: "Shut! Up! Mom! Ughhhh!"

LAUREN: Nope! I didn't want my son to get any crazy ideas. Instead we trudge across town to the poorly maintained and poorly lit soccer fields in the mostly black and Latinx neighborhood.

TASHA [*one of the other soccer moms*]: "Hey! What's up?"

LAUREN: Good afternoon.

TASHA: "He on the team?"

LAUREN: Yes. I received an email from the organizers notifying me that today is the first practice.

TASHA: "They betta not have sent no email to my job. I'm not supposed to get non-work stuff. Damn."

BEVERLY: "You know I understand!"

TASHA: "Those socks are so cool."

LAUREN: Thanks! I let him pick them out himself.

LAUREN: At the first practice I felt proud of my choice to diversify his life.

BEVERLY: "Girl, why is your son running like that?"

LAUREN: Oh no! I forget to check to see if he needs new cleats!

TASHA: "What size does he wear?"

LAUREN: Those are a five. So maybe a six?

TASHA: "Big feet for his age." [*To another mom offstage*] "Cynthia! Cynthia? Where did you get Shante's cleats this year? What? [*To* LAUREN] She's crazy. Oh yeah. You know that Walmart over off 183?"

LAUREN: Yes?

TASHA: "Cool. That's the one. Go to the Goodwill next to that Walmart. Girl, they have cleats in almost every size."

BEVERLY: "Yep. That's the best Goodwill in town."

LAUREN [*surprised*]: Oh. OK. Yeah. Of course. I don't know why I didn't think of that. Yeah, the Goodwill next to the Walmart. [*Beat*] I would never think of that. He was wearing hundred-dollar Nikes from Nordstrom.

BEVERLY: "Mommy, can Jamal come to my birthday sleepover?"

LAUREN: Jamal?

BEVERLY: "Jamal. That tall kid at soccer. You know the one with the blond 'fro hawk."

LAUREN: And the bad attitude? Jamal was a beast on the field. He even got taken out of the game for cursing out a ref! [*To son*] Well. I don't know his mom so . . .

BEVERLY: "Why don't you know her? I see you talking with her during the games sometimes."

LAUREN: Yes, but—

BEVERLY: "Why isn't she your friend, Mommy? You know all the kids at my school and their mothers [*uttered loudly under his breath*] and you don't even like them."

LAUREN: I'm sure that she doesn't want her child to stay overnight at a stranger's house.

BEVERLY: "I already spoke to Jamal. His mom said it's cool."

TASHA [*as Jamal's mother*]: "Hey girl, thanks for inviting Jamal to the party. I'm on the night shift Saturday night. I can drop him off at . . . ?"

LAUREN: Six is great! They'll eat some pizza, play video games, and watch a movie.

TASHA: "Cool! Girl, Jamal been dying to watch that zombie movie."

LAUREN: Actually, I think they're planning to watch one of those Harry Potter films.

TASHA: "Um. Oh. OK. So I'll pick him up around six."

LAUREN: That's a little early in the morning.

TASHA: "What? No, six at night! On Sunday. Girl, you know how it is. I need to sleep in and chill after my night shift. Those boys will be having fun anyway. We good?"

LAUREN: Well, I—

TASHA: "Cool! 'Preciate you!"

LAUREN: It was on. Not only would I need the will to survive a night with six ten-year-old boys but I'd have to get through babysitting badass Jamal the following afternoon. After the other kids were picked up so they could head to tutoring or music lessons—

BEVERLY: "Miss?"

LAUREN: Yes, Jamal?

BEVERLY: "Your house is real nice."

LAUREN: Thank you.

BEVERLY: "It's so quiet here."

LAUREN: Usually.

BEVERLY: "You read all them books?"

LAUREN: Most of them, yes.

BEVERLY: "Whoa, I ain't never seen—"

LAUREN: You never saw?

BEVERLY: "Yeah, never seen these many books at somebody's house. If you read them already then why don't you give them to somebody else so they can read them too?"

LAUREN: That's a good question.

BEVERLY: "What are those pieces of paper on your wall for?"

LAUREN: Oh, that's my diploma from college. The other one is my diploma from graduate school.

BEVERLY: "Wow. I didn't know black people went to those schools."

LAUREN: A few of us do.

BEVERLY: "Wow. That's dope. I want to get a couple of those."

LAUREN: "I'm sure you will." [*Beat*] "You want to borrow that book? That's by James Baldwin."

BEVERLY [*reading slowly*]: *Notes of a Native Son.*

LAUREN: When you're a bit older you should read *Manchild in the Promised Land*, *Invisible Man*, *Their Eyes Were Watching God*, *The Bluest Eye*, *The Color Purple*—

BEVERLY: "You got all of them?"

LAUREN: Yes, I do. You can borrow—no, you can have them when you're ready.

BEVERLY: "Cool. Thanks for having me over."

LAUREN: You're very welcome. Thank you for visiting our home.

TASHA [*as son from offstage*]: "Jamal, come on! Show me how to do a header."

BEVERLY: "See you later."

LAUREN: I really hope so.

SCENE 13. BIRDS, BEES, AND BOMBS

LAUREN [*noticing that* TASHA *is looking at her phone in her purse*]: Tasha, I see what you're doing. We agreed that there will be no cell phones at the retreat.

TASHA [*clandestinely eyeing her cell phone*]: Don't worry about my business. Worry about yourself.

BEVERLY: Why don't I pull another question out of the basket?

LAUREN [*to* TASHA]: You don't have to be rude.

TASHA: I'm not being rude.

LAUREN: You just seem uptight.

TASHA: Uptight? Really? Do I?

LAUREN AND BEVERLY: Yes!

TASHA: I'm just checking on something right quick.

LAUREN: Since today is about sharing—

TASHA: OK. OK. Prom night is coming and he said he's planning to ask someone. Today.

LAUREN: Is he seeing someone?

TASHA: Not that I've heard about. I just hope whoever she is says yes. [*Phone pings.*] Wait! [*Reading a text*] He's got a date! He's got a date! His first date.

BEVERLY: Yay!

LAUREN: Wow! Who is it?

TASHA [*reading text*]: I don't know.

[*Shift to future.* TASHA *is speaking to her son.*]

BEVERLY [*as son*]: "Be patient, Mom. Like I told you before, it's a surprise."

TASHA: A surprise. OK. Well, we need to rent you a tux, pick up some nice kicks, rent the limo, shop for a corsage—

BEVERLY: "I'll do that myself. On my own, Mom. I want everything to be perfect for . . . !"

TASHA [*to audience*]: Who is it? Who could it be? I'm just relieved that somebody wants to romance the only black boy in the junior class. Who has he escorted into his adolescent fantasies? Is it a blonde? A wise Latina? A Filipina? Or maybe, just maybe, it's a black girl? [*Fingers crossed*] I pray it's someone that looks like me. It doesn't really matter because he finally has—

BEVERLY: A date!

TASHA: I guess my baby is not a baby anymore.

[*The doorbell rings.* BEVERLY *as the son answers the door.*]

BEVERLY: "Hey! Wow. You look great. Come on in."

[*He's holding his breath in anticipation.*]

"Mom, meet—"

[*Beat.* TASHA *is shocked. For a minute.*]

"Daniel."

[TASHA *takes it all in, as she grows to realize that the past sixteen years just fell into place.*]

TASHA: Good evening, Daniel. It's such a pleasure to finally meet you. Welcome to our home.

SCENE 14. MOVING DAY

LAUREN: These kids grow up so fast.

TASHA: Can you imagine the day when your child finally leaves the nest?

LAUREN [*as college dean at welcome reception*]: "Welcome to Boutique Charming College, the small liberal arts institution with the big heart—and an even bigger endowment!" [*Laughing at own joke*] "We're thrilled that you're joining our community of learners. As you can see from the map, our four hundred-plus acres allow for plenty of freedom."

BEVERLY: Freedom. I've been preparing for this day for nearly two decades.

LAUREN: "Parents, you should be very proud. Your children come to us today with brilliance and energy, and after attending our quaint school for four years (or five years for those who like to get high), they'll be ready to remake the world!"

BEVERLY: As a Panther Mom (not to be confused with a Tiger Mom), I taught my black child to climb every mountain in a world that wants to put shackles on my baby's body and imagination. I've got muscles you can't even see from lifting a ton of coal into the sun every day.

TASHA: And now you have a diamond that sparkles and shines.

LAUREN AND TASHA: Your work is done.

BEVERLY: The house is so quiet. Empty.

TASHA: And clean!

BEVERLY: Who will sit up with me watching movies? Who will I wait up for in the middle of the night?

LAUREN: You will still pray every night for their safety. He is young and black and male. And living out in the world. Those nights are not fit for sleep.

BEVERLY: Is she really ready to be on her own at eighteen?

TASHA: You raised her. Look in the mirror and ask yourself.

BEVERLY: Will I ever be sure?

LAUREN: I just paid off my own loans and now need to borrow money to pay for his college tuition?

TASHA: I'm that little voice inside your head saying if you weren't so hell bent on being a single mom you'd have another income to draw on to pay for this Ivy League dream—

LAUREN: Yeah! I was so busy raising my son, I forgot to find a partner.

TASHA: We all did, but it's going to be all right. It's got to be all right.

BEVERLY: Oh look, her roommate brought decorations for the room. What the hell? That's a Confederate flag.

TASHA: The changing same. The terror and the hope. The dance continues.

BEVERLY: Do you have all your classes?

LAUREN: "Yes, Mom."

TASHA [*dancing*]: You know the steps.

BEVERLY: You got enough money for books?

LAUREN: "Yes, Mom."

TASHA: Two steps forward.

BEVERLY: Keep an eye on that roommate. In fact, here's the number to the local NAACP.

LAUREN: "Yes, Mom. Got it!"

TASHA: Two steps back.

BEVERLY: Should I buy you a school sweatshirt?

TASHA: Not a hoodie!

LAUREN: "I'm good."

TASHA: Slide.

BEVERLY: Text me or better yet call when you feel sad. Alone. Afraid.

LAUREN: "I'm good."

TASHA: Slide.

BEVERLY: Speak up for yourself if your professors say anything crazy.

LAUREN: "I'm good."

TASHA: Two steps forward.

BEVERLY: Respect your body. And everyone else's.

LAUREN: "Ugh! Mom! I'm good."

TASHA: Three steps back.

BEVERLY: Push yourself even when you think you have nothing left. Grit is sometimes more valuable than smarts.

LAUREN: "I'm good."

TASHA: Slide.

BEVERLY: What if something bad happens?

LAUREN: "It's not."

BEVERLY: What if—

LAUREN: "Don't you trust me?"

BEVERLY: Yes, but I don't trust them.

TASHA: Cha Cha Cha.

LAUREN: "I stand here in this dorm room staring into your dark brown eyes and I'm telling you it's gonna be all right. I'm the person you raised. I'm good."

BEVERLY: I want to say, "But being good never saved anybody black in this country." But instead I say—"I've got to hit the road now before it gets too dark."

LAUREN: I want to tell her—"I'm a little afraid to be without you but I'm also excited. I know there are some difficult things coming my way but there's gonna be amazing adventures too." Instead I say, "Be safe driving home. I love you, Mom."

BEVERLY: I want to say—"I've never been prouder than I am right now. Or more afraid." Instead I say, "I love you too."

[*They embrace powerfully.*]

CODA. NEXT

LAUREN: Even though our kids will leave the nest one day—

TASHA: God willing and the creek don't rise!

LAUREN: If we keep this up, we'll never be alone.

TASHA: You're stuck with me!

BEVERLY: For better or worse. For richer, for poorer.

TASHA: 'Til death do us part!

LAUREN: You always gotta take it there, Tasha!

[*They all laugh.*]

OK, ladies. The chef has prepared a yummy dinner for us this evening. Remember this is a planning dinner. [*To the audience*] We need volunteers to organize the Mother's Day Brunch and a few more selections for our summer book club. Any other announcements?

[TASHA *raises her hand.*]

Yes, Tasha.

TASHA: Thank you, Madame President! OK, I want to remind everyone that at next month's meeting there will be a shoe swap. Make sure you bring those shoes that are too tight for your bunions. Don't shake your head, I know you have more than a few pairs to contribute, Stacey!

LAUREN: Thank you, Tasha. Newcomers, we always end our meetings with a little tradition. Let's all join hands and recite the BBSM mantra. New members, please note that it is printed at the bottom of the retreat agenda. Got it? All together now.

ALL: We are proud Black single mothers and with our strong sisterhood behind us there's nothing we can't do.

[LAUREN, BEVERLY, *and* TASHA *hug and then say good-bye to each other and to the audience members.*]

INTERVIEW WITH THE PLAYWRIGHT

Joan Morgan

This conversation about *Underground, Monroe, and The Mamalogues: Three Plays* was conducted by telephone on May 16, 2019. It has been condensed and edited for clarity.

So, what a great body of work, Lisa Thompson. You should feel really good about that.

Thank you so much.

So, this is where I wanted to start. I know that Single Black Female *is not in the book, but that is where I encountered your work for the first time, I want to say, in the early 2000s. Do you remember?*

Yes! I said, "Oh my God, I made it. Joan Morgan knows who I am!" [Laughter.]

I think that was 2004, 2006. I remember I came with Mitzi Miller and I just remember feeling like someone really gets us. You dedicate this book to black girl storytellers. And thirteen years later, the climate for black girl storytellers is so different than it was in 2006, right? And in 2006, it was even far more different than it was in 1976 and 1977, when Ntozake Shange starts to become a presence in our lives. There's such an interesting Bay Area thread between you and Ntozake and Issa Rae. Y'all are like Bay Area babies.

That's true.

You and Issa Rae both spent time on the Farm, our beloved Stanford. Let's start with place. What do you think the Bay Area has given now three gen-

erations of boss-ass storytellers? What do you think it is about place that has influenced this storytelling ability? It's really fascinating to me that you all are from Northern California.

I had not thought about that—that's why I wanted to speak with you, because you recognize trends that most people would not identify. One thing I'm interested in depicting is the experience of black Californians, particularly those of us from the Bay Area. When I applied to graduate school, I proposed a two-part project—a documentary and a cultural studies dissertation about black San Francisco—because I realized it was disappearing. I changed my project. It became a study about black middle-class women's sexuality that resulted in my first play, *Single Black Female*, and my book, *Beyond the Black Lady: Sexuality and the New Black Middle Class*, which is based on my dissertation. But black California is always in my heart. I do believe that black people in California have a freedom that is not available to other people in other places because we're literally at the land's end (on the left coast). There is not as much lore about us and our world. I want to explore what it means to be a black Californian in a way that hasn't been articulated before. We have a particular experience. There is a lot of freedom, and some loneliness too, because we're somewhat isolated. Until I visited Brooklyn in my twenties, I didn't realize that some groups of black people didn't get along with each other, I had no idea that folks from different parts of the African Diaspora clashed. That was all new to me!

You were like, "There are enough of you to do that?"

Exactly! So, there is a creative freedom that comes from isolation. If I do place myself as a representative of the generation between Issa Rae and Shange (who is the mother of it all), I'd argue that quality of freedom allowed us to be disruptive and innovative storytellers: Shange's invention of the choreopoem, my use of surreal vignettes, and Rae's use of new media. There is a freedom to dream, to experiment and be the kind of storyteller that comes out of that particularly Northern California experience. Although Issa Rae was raised in Los Angeles and Shange grew up in St. Louis and New Jersey, they both spent foundational time in the cauldron that is the Bay Area.

Because she left us so recently, I think a lot of us are reflecting on what Ntozake's legacy means, not just in our lives but in our work. I'm wondering if you can speak a little bit about what she means to you. You have to tell me if you performed in For Colored Girls, *because I feel like every black girl in my gen has. If you have, then what color lady were you?*

I first read her play in middle school. I heard the advertisements for *For Colored Girls* on KDIA, Oakland's black radio station. I still remember hearing the actor passionately saying, "I have loved you assiduously for eight months, two weeks, and a day." I pleaded with my mom to take me to see it. She said, "No, you're too young, and I don't want you to have bad ideas about black men." I was so disappointed. She wouldn't let me do it, so I read the play instead. I told my best friend's mother, "I'm going to be the Ntozake of my generation." She looked at me, blew smoke in my eyes, and said, "You ain't gonna do shit." Wasn't that cold? My friends would hang out in my bedroom and I would recite it to them all the time. I don't think I've ever seen a proper performance of it, but I performed monologues all the time with my friends. Wait! I did a *For Colored Girls* monologue for class with Anna Deavere Smith at UCLA. It was the "Sorry" monologue by the Lady in Red.

Shange, along with Nikki Giovanni, Sonia Sanchez, and many other black women writers, gave me permission to tell the truth in ways that the moms in my neighborhood did not give me. I would go to the San Francisco public library and read their books. They told me, you have a voice, and you need to use it to tell the story of girls like you. So, they were the literary mothers that raised me. And I ended up in a class with Ntozake when I was a senior at UCLA! The first time I wrote a monologue was in her class. She told us to write something on the first day. I wrote nonstop, channeling this character who I understood so well—a black woman with a broken heart. She asked who wants to read their work, and I stood up. When I read it to the class I realized, "Oh my god, I'm a playwright"—because up until that point, I considered myself a poet. Being in her class taught me that I could still keep the poetry but use it in a different way.

Now that we talked about you and Ntozake, what is the connective thread you see between yourself and your early work and Issa Rae? I just keep thinking what would happen if Single Black Female *was being written now. Can you talk to us about change and climate in the context of your work? What has changed, what remains the same, what are you excited about for young black storytellers, and what do you think some of the same challenges are? What's the connective thread you see?*

That's a very rich question. For one, it's wonderful that younger storytellers have people like Shonda Rhimes and Larry Wilmore (co-creator, *Insecure*), blazing a clear path for Issa Rae to follow. In 2004, when *Single Black Female* had its L.A. run, HBO looked at it. At that time, there wasn't a visible major black producer in episodic TV that I could look to with significant power to support the project.

As an audience member, I devour all the stuff that's being done now. I really love *Random Acts of Flyness*, I love *Insecure*. I love watching all this stuff, but I do long for images of black folks who are not in their twenties and thirties. You get a little bit of that with *Queen Sugar*, but I'm hungry for more. I was actually always hungry for that even when I was in my twenties because I really love being around folks from multiple generations. Hopefully, there will be stories about life and love told by and about black people over forty. I have some projects that I created that present that viewpoint. Maybe we will see them on screen.

Let's talk about the scholarly aspect of your life for a little bit. I think that's what is really unique about you in many ways. There are some other folk, like E. Patrick Johnson, but generally the writer-scholar trajectory is someone who has been a writer first for a while, and then decides they're going to go get some stability in their lives and get a Ph.D., some health insurance. And you've really done them concurrently. Why?

Insanity, hard-headedness. I was really torn about which path to follow, being an artist or being a scholar. I went to law school for a few months but I hated it. I went back to UCLA for a master's in African American studies. I was still trying to figure out what to do next when I wrote a one-woman show called *Dreadtime Stories*. I performed it at the Inner City Cultural Center's Talent Fest, and it went really well; I advanced to the finals but realized I didn't want to be a performer. I talked to my advisor, Valerie Smith; she was like, "Do both!" and I was like, "She's crazy." Shortly after that I applied to graduate schools. Then, after walking into my classroom at my first job, I felt so at peace and knew that it was something I was meant to do. *Single Black Female* premiered when I was a grad student, and it went really well. That's when I started wondering, "So, what if you're actually good at two things?" They both feature different parts of your soul, and in each one you hide Easter eggs of the other. In my creative work, I embed lots of African American history and culture, whether it's an address that has significance, a date, or the name of a character.

When I'm teaching cultural studies courses, I make sure students are allowed to be creative. That means doing visual art, short films or videos, plays, poems, photography. I give them freedom to do what I wasn't given license to do but did anyway as an undergraduate and graduate student. I always wanted to create and respond to intellectual work in a creative way. I want to give my students a place to do that. It's really important for me to bring my artist self to the classroom. I'm going to write an essay about that. I think it is important pedagogically, because people demonstrate their intelligence in different ways. I don't think bubbling in a Scantron sheet gives me enough information about what you're getting out of class. The same goes for writing an essay. Students should be allowed, even encouraged, to do other things to demonstrate what they've learned. I love to see engineering and biology majors write their first play or poem. It's amazing.

It wasn't an easy choice. Some of my friends have gone on to do great things, like winning Tony Awards and other amazing stuff, and I wondered where I'd be if I'd stuck with just being an artist. Then I realized my "ministry" is more than one thing. It doesn't make me better or special, it's just me. I'm at peace with that now. It does mean it takes longer to get things done because you're trying to please two different groups, the academic world and the theater world. But I think that I am at a place now in my life that I can accept that duality, and thrive as both an artist and a scholar. I call it dancing on the slash. I no longer look at it as my work being divided. There is a porous line between my art and scholarship, and I work within that space.

Lisa, the topic of class comes up repeatedly in both your plays and actually your scholarly work also. What is it about black folks and class that you're trying to figure out in the work?

I'm just fascinated by class and race, and I always have been. I found out that we weren't solidly middle-class when I met a black woman in the dorms who was a debutante. She lived literally on the other side of the tracks from me in San Francisco, literally the BART tracks divided us. One of her parents came to visit, then sent a thank-you note, and I was blown away. I remember she had this beautiful Laura Ashley comforter. I didn't know what a comforter was—and a pillow sham? Nope.

That class, particularly the black middle class, seems to be a recurring theme in your work, and I was wondering if you could talk about it, in both your scholarly work and your plays.

I didn't really understand my own class position until college. I'm still thinking about what it means to have class ascension. As a first-generation, college-educated person—I'm in no way fetishizing that kind of knowledge—you quickly understand cultural capital and the access it provides. It's a peculiar experience being in close proximity to certain kinds of wealth, power, and true cultural capital. You often find yourself walking a tightrope as an African American, navigating these privileged spaces.

It's important to discuss how notions of class in the African American community have changed over the years. I teach a course that examines cultural representations of the black middle class and have my students work through Du Bois's "Talented Tenth," E. Franklin Frazier's *Black Bourgeoisie*, and Trey Ellis's "New Black Aesthetic." Those three texts cover a hundred-year period. The black middle class are presented as either saviors or sell-outs until you get to the end of the twentieth century. Now, in the early twenty-first century, they're considered just another group of black people struggling to make sense of their peculiar position within the American racial and class hierarchy. I'm so fascinated by class because of my own family's journey. My son mostly encounters black people with Ph.D.s, like his parents. I'm in between these two generations: my parents who never finished college, and my son who sees college as a given. At the same time, all of us, no matter where we are on the spectrum of class, navigate those moments of black trauma, the murder of our children, the mistreatment of black girls in schools, all these horrific things that also make up being black. You could be returning from your vacation on Martha's Vineyard, but you're still worried about being pulled over by the police on the way home from the airport.

I think that that's really fascinating in the work, too, particularly if you look at Underground *and* Monroe. *They are definitely about the desires to have some sort of class ascension as escape. But they're also as much about what is the appropriate response to continuous black trauma. And those things are in really wonderful tension. Confessional note, I'm Jamaican and so it's amazing to me how class is so not a discussion in the United States, but is so clearly present in everything. It's always a discussion in Jamaican culture; there is no pretending that class doesn't matter. I'm wondering what is it about the condition of blackness in America that so often puts those things into conversation. Black trauma, and what the solution to it should be, and black ascension, and whether that is a solution or if it's actually a detriment to curing the trauma, resolving the trauma.*

It's a constant challenge for us. To give into or buy into the American dream, or the capitalist dream across countries, is to embrace this notion of ascension that in some ways you're assuming or hoping will provide some sort of prophylactic, some measure of protection. And, I think, in some ways it does. What happened to Henry Louis Gates Jr. is only possible because of who he is—he ends up in the White House. That's my interest, that peculiar moment—of course, if he isn't who he is, it's another tragic story, it's different because he's a famous Harvard professor. So, I am clear that certain kinds of situations are made easier. But I think there's also frustration. Larry Bobo had a study that looked at black people's attitudes in L.A. after the riots. Black middle-class people were angrier than working-class and poor black people. The anger was greater among the privileged. So, I think it's clearly not an escape, it's not a guarantee of anything but better seats on the plane. We're all going in the same direction. You're mad that you paid more money for the seat, but you're still going to the same place. I'm glad this current generation is thinking about it but not feeling shame for being middle-class or trying to conceal their middle-class background, nor are they lording it over other people. It's still not perfect by any means, but I think people are thinking about class and privilege more. I hope the younger generation is more clear-eyed about what this does—the price of the ticket is very high, but what they're actually getting for their ticket . . .

I was going to ask you if you think that this younger generation has a different relationship to class and cultural mulatto-ness than let's say, our generation, the generation Trey Ellis is writing about in "The New Black Aesthetic."

I definitely do. I think that they're much more free . . . I'm going to pat our generation on the back and say that we gave them this moment. You don't have a Terence Nance without a George C. Wolfe or without a Trey Ellis giving birth to this theory. It's a broadening of that idea among these new black cultural producers and others who are willing to put themselves out there. I mean, we don't talk about it, but they depict black queer folks, gay, lesbian, trans, and bisexual characters. These young folks are like, you have to come out as straight now. And I love that. So, I think they are more comfortable. They're enjoying the fruits of the seeds our generation sowed.

What do you think are some of the tropes that this generation and the upcoming generation of storytellers are going to be trying to work out, particularly black women?

That's a great question. What I see happening is a broadening of the story of black womanhood. It is so wonderful to see all these stories by and about black women. They came here, whether they were born on the African continent and have grown up in the U.S. or they were born here to parents that immigrated when they were in college or in grad school and raised them. Black women are talking about their experiences as black women who are part of the diaspora in a different way. I'm seeing work recognizing trans black women and their stories. I created my first trans character recently. It was part of this show that was curated by Dominique Morisseau, *50in50: Letters to Our Daughters*, monologues by black women for black women. I wanted to talk about mothering from the viewpoint of a trans mother who does not give birth to her trans daughter but stands in as a mother figure. I heard that Angelica Ross from *Pose* actually read that monologue at the NYC show! I think there's a bigger idea of what black womanhood is. And you've helped me with that definitely, seeing your work, and how you talk about black womanhood. I think that the new generation is also getting a lot from folks that have broken that space open, so that one day we won't worry about who the "authentic" black woman is, because it's already assumed that there's a wide variety of black women. I do think we all dream about many of the same things—joy, safety, love, and freedom—but come to it in different ways.

Let's turn back to place. What do you think Austin, in particular, gave these works, these three plays?

It's kind of crazy to me that those three plays ended up being produced in Austin. Today, I was looking at photos of me and my son when we first came here seven years ago. The artistic community embraced me and my work. There are a lot of amazing, talented actors here, but unfortunately they eventually leave. They cut their teeth in Austin and then they head to New York, L.A., or Chicago, and then they blow up. Director Rudy Ramirez has been really instrumental in making sure to get my work up in Austin, especially at The Vortex, which is a hub for new and innovative work. In general, Austin is an amazing incubator, and I'm so happy that the audience has responded so well. I'm especially pleased about those who are coming to the theater for the first time to see work by a black woman.

UT Austin was the first place to hire me as both a scholar and an artist. The department wanted me to bring both parts of myself. I wasn't doing playwriting on the side: it is an integral part of my teaching and cultural curating. I've been able to bring in black theater and performance artists to work with my students and to share their work with the community, so it's been a pretty remarkable place for me.

You are the biggest disrupter of the idea that "those who can't teach . . ."

Thank you! A few years ago, I gave a talk on *BlackademicsTV* that challenges that idea. I actually want to find a way to spotlight the people who are doing just that, teaching and doing. I would love to either edit an anthology or create some kind of video series to look at people who are doing both. I'm really unapologetic about that. I'm award-winning in all three areas: teaching, scholarship, and playwriting. I understand that I'm privileged to be able to do that. Part of it is being stubborn. I wanted to do it because I wasn't supposed to do it. I refuse to believe that people who are artists can't teach well. Some of my best teachers have been artists, such as Ntozake Shange, Anna Deavere Smith, and Cherríe Moraga. The idea that people who are scholars can't be artists is such a lie.

So, what's the dream project? What's next?

I want to finish my Great Migration trilogy that begins with *Monroe*. The second installment about the migration from the South to California is called *Gold*, and it's set in San Francisco. The final installment (which is unnamed) will be about someone moving down south as part of the reverse migration. So, that one will mirror my own journey. It will explore what it means to be a child of migrants who returns to the region of their parents' birth after they've passed away. Also, I'd love to collaborate with musicians and dancers on a project. I now realize that it's all about creating work with people that you respect and care for. Having a career as a scholar provides stability, so I can chase the art, not the check. I tell my students all the time that if you love what you're doing, the money will follow, because people follow the light. You will be the light when you are doing what you love. People are just drawn to that light, and other things that come from that . . . the wonderful ways in which it allows you to build community—which is more important than money. It's a beautiful thing. I can't believe the life I've built.

It is a beautiful thing. Is there anything else that you really want to talk about that I didn't ask you?

There's something I would tell all of the little black girls writing. Keep writing. I think about that little black girl who grew up in San Francisco, and I want to tell her you have many stories to tell. I wrote all the time; I thought it was just self-indulgent, but all of it is work. You're sharpening your tool. It's a gift and you must honor it, and honor the people that share it with you, the other artists in your life and also those that are being fed from it because you're being fed from them too. I'm so glad I got to talk about all of this with you.

I'm really happy to be able to do it. Thank you for choosing me. Like I said, what an impressive body of work. And I love that I really came to you first as a playwright, that I didn't know anything about you as a scholar.

That's wonderful. Now we are part of each other's community. That journey is beautiful.